weBELONG

ASCD MEMBER BOOK

Many ASCD members received this book as a
member benefit upon its initial release.

Learn more at: **www.ascd.org/memberbooks**

Laurie Barron • Patti Kinney

50 Strategies to Create Community and Revolutionize Classroom Management

ascd

Alexandria, Virginia USA

1703 N. Beauregard St. • Alexandria, VA 22311-1714 USA
Phone: 800-933-2723 or 703-578-9600 • Fax: 703-575-5400
Website: www.ascd.org • Email: member@ascd.org
Author guidelines: www.ascd.org/write

Ranjit Sidhu, *CEO & Executive Director;* Penny Reinart, *Chief Impact Officer;* Genny Ostertag, *Senior Director, Acquisitions and Editing;* Susan Hills, *Acquisitions Editor;* Julie Houtz, *Director, Book Editing;* Katie Martin, *Editor;* Thomas Lytle, *Creative Director;* Donald Ely, *Art Director;* Georgia Park, *Graphic Designer;* Valerie Younkin, *Senior Production Designer;* Shajuan Martin, *E-Publishing Specialist;* Kelly Marshall, *Production Manager;* Christopher Logan, *Senior Production Specialist*

PAPERBACK ISBN: 978-1-4166-3026-5   ASCD product #122002
PDF E-BOOK ISBN: 978-1-4166-3027-2; see Books in Print for other formats.

Quantity discounts are available: email programteam@ascd.org or call 800-933-2723, ext. 5773, or 703-575-5773. For desk copies, go to www.ascd.org/deskcopy.

ASCD Member Book No. F21-8 (July 2021, PSI+). ASCD Member Books mail to Premium (P), Select (S), and Institutional Plus (I+) members on this schedule: Jan, PSI+; Feb, P; Apr, PSI+; May, P; Jul, PSI+; Aug, P; Sep, PSI+; Nov, PSI+; Dec, P. For current details on membership, see www.ascd.org/membership.

Library of Congress Cataloging-in-Publication Data

Names: Barron, Laurie, author. | Kinney, Patti, 1952- author.
Title: We belong : 50 strategies to create community and revolutionize
    classroom management / Laurie Barron & Patti Kinney.
Description: Alexandria, Virginia USA : ASCD, [2021] | Includes
    bibliographical references and index.
Identifiers: LCCN 2021014042 (print) | LCCN 2021014043 (ebook) | ISBN
    9781416630265 (paperback) | ISBN 9781416630272 (pdf)
Subjects: LCSH: Classroom management. | Social learning. | Teacher-student
    relationships. | Communication in education.
Classification: LCC LB3013 .B337 2021 (print) | LCC LB3013 (ebook) | DDC
    371.102/4—dc23
LC record available at https://lccn.loc.gov/2021014042
LC ebook record available at https://lccn.loc.gov/2021014043

30 29 28 27 26 25 24 23 22 21   1 2 3 4 5 6 7 8 9 10 11 12

we BELONG

Downloadable Tools

Reproducible copies of the following resources, discussed in text, are available as a free PDF at **http://www.ascd.org/we-belong-122002**.

Foreword

Throughout my many years as a middle-level teacher, I have come to understand that successful classroom management is rooted in building relationships with the students who walk through my door. Young adolescents are arguably the most difficult group of students to corral into some sort of organized chaos. For any teacher, fostering relationships and increasing belonging is critical but complex. What helps immensely when you're faced with a formidable student determined to challenge your authority? An arsenal of thoughtful and practical strategies.

Over the years, I've encountered my share of memorable students. I'm thinking of H. T., who proudly entered my classroom not only swearing, "I don't do math," but also bragging, "It won't matter anyway. I will be back in lockup soon." I'm also thinking of D. T., the 14-year-old 6th grader whose reputation with local law enforcement preceded him. And then there's B. G., who calls me every swear word (coupled with my name) that I've ever heard and even taught me a few new ones.

I would love to say these remarkable young people were unusual, but nothing with teaching is truly predictable or extraordinary. The middle and high school years are tumultuous for the easiest of pre-adolescents and adolescents, and they're downright torture for some of the rest. But with the right tools, a teacher can find ways to make headway with every student. All of my experience has taught me that helping students fit in and feel connected is the key to their success and the success of a classroom.

The key for H. T.? I let him sit in front of the room, next to me. He loved being "in charge," helping me, and having me nearby to help him. I discovered that he never ate lunch. So I kept cheese sticks, granola bars, and apple juice on hand for him to quietly grab when needed. This made a world of difference in his personality and behavior.

Reaching D. T. was harder, and I am sad to say that I never found the key to unlock his protective armor. How I wish that I'd had a resource like this book back then. I see in it a variety of new strategies I could have tried with him and many other students. Unfortunately, D. T. was unable to escape the school-to-prison pipeline, and 20 years later, I still feel responsible for not helping him find the sense of belonging that he needed—and that might have changed the trajectory of his life.

B. G. and I still have our ups and downs, but the two of us have found ways to help her cope with her struggles to fit in. The key for her? A network of peers who model appropriate classroom behaviors. This helped B. G. feel that she belonged. It also helped her manage her behaviors, which let other students view her as a contributing member of our classroom.

The point of these vignettes is that each child is different. Every one of them walks through your classroom door with a unique set of insecurities and baggage and their own "combination lock." Deciphering that combination can be difficult. But if a teacher has a stock of strategies, the possibilities for unlocking good relationships and successful learning are endless. A book like *We Belong* can help you refine and organize practices you may have used in the past and teach you new strategies you can easily insert into any blank spots in tomorrow's plans.

❖ ❖ ❖

When I first met Patti Kinney through the National Middle School Association, we were both part of a listserv (yes, that is how old-school people did things) called "MiddleTalk." Teachers posed questions about teaching adolescents and offered one another answers in long threads of discussion. Patti's voice was one I followed and respected. Over the years, we have bumped into each other in many virtual settings, and I have been a fan of her writings and thoughts. Her book *Voices of Experience: Perspectives from Successful Middle Level Leaders* touched me with its honesty and insights into middle-level education. Patti introduced me to Laurie Barron, whose wisdom I have come to value. Her expertise informs the professional development opportunities she provides to teachers and school leaders everywhere. These two outstanding educators collaborated on *Middle*

School: A Place to Belong and Become, a book that has been the trusted guide for my classroom structure since it was published in 2018. The weaving of their individual experiences creates a readable, usable text. I've reached for it so often that the pages are already dog-eared and filled with notes.

I've repeatedly referred to middle school students because they have been the focus of my professional life. However, I've always felt that, if a strategy can work with this age group, it can work with any students! This book does a fantastic job of embracing a wide span of teachers and learners, offering ways to apply the suggested strategies to different grade levels and subject areas. For example, the section on Daily Agendas demonstrates three different ways to adapt the strategy. Any teacher would be able to use the examples in his or her own classroom with ease.

One of my favorite gems mined from this book is Strategy 42: "Help students make friends with failure." Many of a teacher's biggest behavior challenges are from students who feel "dumb"; because they believe that they are not ever going to be academically successful, they choose to act out instead of continuing to try. Strategy 42 outlines ways to find an inroad with those students, by getting them to understand that failure is a part of *all* of us and that it is a natural part of success and learning. I love the suggestions offered here to help students overcome their fears. Another favorite is Strategy 8: "Build belonging with relationship promises." I love the list of promises and the suggestion to review it and repeat the promises to yourself monthly over the school year. I know that I need an occasional pick-me-up boost to remind myself of the importance of all those small things that help build and maintain good teacher–student relationships.

In today's world, with limitless free information at our fingertips and countless "experts" begging us to try out their philosophies, selling a book is a tough task. Like many, I only want to spend my money on something that will be worthy of a hallowed spot on my small desktop bookshelf. *We Belong* is a book that will make it into that limited space. It's a rich text, full of practical advice, encouragement, checklists, and strategies; I plan to fill it with sticky notes, margin comments, and highlights. I'll reach for it again and again when I start a new school year and anytime I am feeling challenged by students in my class.

Writing a foreword feels a bit like writing an advertisement. But in reality, it is more of a book-club conversation between you and me. I want you to experience the promise and excitement I felt when I finished this book. I know these insights and ideas can help rejuvenate your practices. I'm sure that this revitalization will help your students feel that they are part of a *we*—individually accepted members of a supported, valued community. Their sense of belonging, in turn, will help you with all the organizational, relational, and behavioral challenges of classroom management.

—Cossondra George
Veteran Middle School Teacher

Introduction:
Belonging and Classroom
Management—A Dynamic
Partnership

It begins before they enter the school building.

As soon as students board the bus or set foot on the school grounds, they start picking up signals about whether or not they fit in. These signals come from peers, teachers, other school staff members, or other students' family members on the school grounds. Perceptions accumulate as students pass through the halls and other communal areas of the school (including bathrooms, locker rooms, the gym, the cafeteria) and into their classrooms. Impressions about the extent of their *belongingness* continue to pile up throughout the day, and these affect students' comfort and enjoyment in school, as well as the ways in which they view themselves, one another, and their successes in and out of the classroom. Combined, these impressions influence students' behavior and the ways they respond to their teachers and fellow classmates. This signal-gathering is repeated every school day.

From the moment their feet hit the school grounds to the moment they leave, students' experiences of belonging (or *not* belonging) powerfully intertwine with the dynamics of their classrooms, affecting the overall school culture and each student's learning experience. It's time to acknowledge belonging as a major component of school life and a major consideration of classroom management.

What Belonging Is

Belonging is the perception one has of being accepted, valued, and included in a particular group or setting. To be socially connected is a fundamental human need—one that goes beyond just a need for social interaction. Every human needs to be part of a group in which connections are genuine, caring, and ongoing (DeWall, Deckman, Pond, & Bonser, 2011; Maslow, 1968; Osterman, 2000).

School belonging has been described as "the extent to which students feel personally accepted, respected, included, and supported by others in the school social environment" (Goodenow & Grady, 1993, p. 80). Schools offer multiple and unique social situations for young people to develop a sense of belonging—or, conversely, to have their sense of belonging thwarted. Thus, schools are critical settings for attending to the need to belong. Across grade levels, a sense of belonging in the school or classroom positively affects a variety of social, emotional, and academic variables. Its importance grows to particular intensity in the middle and high school grades (Blum & Libbey, 2004; Goodenow, 1993a, 1993b; Steinberg & Monahan, 2007).

According to belonging theorists Baumeister and Leary (1995),

> This is more than the need for social contact or for multiple acquaintances within the classroom or school. The need to belong is for ongoing, positive, comfortable bonds that are stable and that the student has reason to believe will continue. They don't have to wonder every day if the good feeling they had yesterday will be dashed today. (p. 500)

Why Belonging in School Matters

Belonging may be a feeling, but it manifests in tangible ways. A growing body of research and theory related to school belonging (or school connectedness) concludes that belonging has a host of positive personal, social, and academic benefits (Allen, Kern, Vella-Brodrick, Hattie, & Waters, 2016; Juvonen, 2006; Klem & Connell, 2004; Lee & Robbins, 1998; Loukas, Roalson, & Herrera, 2010; Maddox & Prinz, 2003; O'Neel & Fuligni, 2013; Shochet, Dadds, Ham, & Montague, 2006; Wang & Holcombe, 2010). A sense of belonging generally leads to increases in the following:

- Positive, prosocial classroom behavior
- Attendance rates

- Self-esteem
- Self-confidence
- Self-belief
- Optimism
- Positive peer relationships
- Classroom engagement
- Focus on academic tasks
- Academic achievement
- School satisfaction
- Positive attitudes toward school and learning
- Skills of self-management
- Resilience to deal with crises
- Buffer against effects of a negative home environment

Belonging is such a basic need that the *lack* of it can lead to "dire consequences" (Baumeister & Leary, 1995) and, consequently, difficult classroom management situations. Students who feel confused, isolated, rejected, demeaned, ignored, or excluded are at high risk for a variety of social, emotional, and academic difficulties (Anderman, 2002; Baumeister & Leary, 1995; Baumeister, DeWall, Ciarocco, & Twenge, 2005; Baumeister, Twenge, & Nuss, 2002; Furrer & Skinner, 2003; Leets & Wolf, 2005; Loukas et al., 2010; Osterman, 2000; Resnick et al., 1997; Twenge, Baumeister, DeWall, Ciarocco, & Bartels, 2007).

When students do *not* feel a sense of belonging at school (or are not sure that they belong), they can experience the following:

- Anxiety
- Emotional distress
- Anger and frustration
- Erosion of self-worth
- Lack of self-confidence
- Loneliness
- Helplessness
- Powerlessness
- Incidence of risky behaviors
- Incidence of antisocial connections
- Behavior or conduct problems

- Behavioral and psychological stress
- Distraction from learning tasks
- Disconnection from the group and group activities
- Difficulties with self-management
- Declines in academic performance
- Alienation from learning activities
- Inability to resist undesirable impulses
- Inability to follow protocols
- Susceptibility to self-defeating behavior
- Social avoidance behaviors

How to Increase Belongingness

Here's the good news: educators can help students gain and enjoy a sense of belonging in classrooms and schools. There is concrete evidence that intentional practices and plans to increase belonging do make a difference—not only boosting the sense of membership in the group but also promoting the other benefits of belonging we've described and leading to a more harmonious and positive classroom environment (Anderman & Freeman, 2004; Blum & Libbey, 2004; U.S. Centers for Disease Control and Prevention [CDC], 2009).

So how do we do this? What factors must we consider and what actions must we take to shape our classrooms into places that generate a sense of comfortable membership for all students? The work begins with familiarizing ourselves with the critical school and classroom conditions that contribute to a sense of belonging (Juvonen, 2006; Libbey, 2004, 2007; Resnick et al., 1997; U.S. CDC, 2009; Wingspread, 2004):

- **A safe environment that communicates an authentic sense of caring, trust, and inclusion among all members.** Here, students see evidence that others care about them personally and receive respectful treatment from adults and peers. They are free from experiences of being demeaned, embarrassed, or excluded.
- **Clearly communicated, consistently observed, and equitably enforced behavioral and academic expectations.** Students receive help

in developing skills of self-regulation and management, emotional control, and coping, as well as assistance identifying their own inner resources. They are taught both the social skills needed for satisfying school connections and schoolwork and the academic skills needed to navigate school successfully. They learn to set, manage, and accomplish goals.

- **Access to autonomous experiences and successful engagement in relevant, personalized learning endeavors.** Students are able to take part in planning, carrying out, and evaluating their own schoolwork, and they are offered choices and given opportunities to express their ideas, opinions, and feedback. They also learn to work with others to complete tasks, create things, make decisions, solve problems, and manage crises.

Many of these factors encompass the social-emotional learning "core competencies" of self-awareness, self-management, social awareness, relationship skills, and responsible decision making (see CASEL, 2020a). By working with students to build these skills, teachers can advance a host of social-emotional practices that contribute to a more positive classroom environment.

Classroom Management—and the Difference It Makes

Classroom management can be defined as the strategies and attitudes through which a teacher organizes and operates the classroom environment in order to provide the best possible setting for academic and social-emotional learning. The term describes the whole of how the class functions, the relationships and interactions within the classroom, how everyone works together, and how students learn. Classroom management is a top concern for many teachers, and there's no wonder why: it's a thread that runs through everything that happens once the bell rings and knits it all into a unified whole. The classroom climate teachers create is the vessel that holds the seeds of belonging and provides the space and inputs belonging needs to flourish.

Classroom management and belonging are a dynamic duo. They go hand in hand, nurturing and fueling each other. It's a relationship that's lively, full of adjustment and progress. And it's genuinely difficult for one to thrive without the other.

On the one hand, the elements of classroom management directly affect the sense of belonging (or not belonging) for every individual in the group. These elements include such factors and practices as

- Classroom setting, schedule, organization, and protocols
- Expectations for the ways people treat one another
- Teaching and practicing appropriate behavior
- Development of student self-regulation
- Communication and relationships within the classroom
- Appropriateness and implementation of consequences; responses to problems and issues
- Ways students participate in and contribute to classroom life
- Learning plans and instructional practices

On the other hand, and simultaneously, the extent to which students feel they belong (or doubt they belong) influences these same elements of classroom management. When students learn and practice skills of belonging (and of helping others to belong), many aspects of classroom management work more smoothly. For example:

- Students who see themselves as fully equal and accepted members of the group have less need to be defiant or disruptive.
- The more students get signals that they belong, the less energy they will expend trying to belong or suffering anxiety about not belonging.
- The more students belong, the more their energies are freed to focus on learning tasks.
- The more often students have the communal experience of working together harmoniously for a shared goal—and accomplishing that goal together—the more likely they are to get along with one another.
- The more they feel respected and valued as students, the more their talents shine.
- The more students feel included, the less self-doubt impedes their productivity.
- In the presence of teachers and peers who believe every student can meet expectations, they have more self-belief and confidence as students—and they work harder and care more about academic skills.

- The more students participate in something they care about, the more positive and cooperative their behavior becomes in general.
- The more students feel trusted, the more likely they are to be agreeable and cooperative.

As part of its efforts to address health risks and behaviors, the CDC (U.S. CDC, 2009) identified school connectedness as a promising factor in protecting against factors that can adversely affect health, behavior, and education outcomes for children and adolescents. One of the CDC's six key strategies to increase school connectedness is "effective classroom management and teaching methods to foster a positive learning environment" (2009, p. 9). Other studies support the claim that effective, positive classroom management is critical in any efforts to increase belonging and form a positive classroom group (Allen & Bowles, 2012; McNeely, Nonnemaker, & Blum, 2002; Osterman, 2010; Wingspread, 2004).

So what are the "effective classroom management and teaching methods" that foster a positive learning environment? What does such management look like in practice? It may be a picture that differs from what you think of when you hear the words "classroom management." Think beyond protocols and procedures that make operations run smoothly or ensure that the teacher has control and that students follow the codes of conduct. Think of a far broader definition of *management*—a mix of organization and consistency with the best of social-emotional learning practices (see Battistich & Horn, 1997; Blum, McNeely, & Rinehart, 2002; McNeely et al., 2002; Ryan & Patrick, 2001; U.S. CDC, 2009). It includes the following:

- The prioritization of emotional, social, and physical safety
- Consistent protocols and routines
- Clear guidelines
- Good organization and planning
- An emphasis on positive, respectful, and supportive relationships
- Demonstration (by adults) of trust and belief in students
- The practice of mutual respect
- Student-centered and democratic procedures and learning experiences
- A discipline climate that is not harsh or punitive
- Fair, consistent consequences
- Consistent attitudes toward and treatment of all students
- Trustworthy teachers

- A high value on learning
- Effective, relevant, and engaging instructional practices
- A hearty dose of fun and laughter

If a classroom lacks the attributes of safe, effective, organized, caring, democratic management, students' individual sense of belonging will be thwarted or seriously harmed. If students feel unequal or unworthy, if classroom life is chaotic and unpredictable, if learning activities are poorly planned and protocols unclear, if expectations or consequences are inconsistent, if students feel little involvement in or responsibility for their own learning—it will be hard for students to feel they belong.

When students feel they belong, they participate more and behave better. When students are free to grow as persons—to learn, to find their strengths, and to invest in positive relationships and academic interests—things just run more smoothly in the classroom. When your classroom workings are intentionally well organized and well planned, and your classroom culture is caring, civil, and uplifting, everyone feels valued and gives value to everyone else. Cooperation is practiced and respected, and students' sense of belonging thrives. The partnership of effective, positive classroom management and a focus on the skills of belonging result in social, emotional, and academic learning at their best.

How to Combine Belonging and Classroom Management in Practice

Good, positive management will always be beneficial, but on its own it's not enough to make the kind of headway on belonging that students need for an optimal school experience. To do that, teachers and schools must take the following deliberate actions:

1. Use classroom management practices that establish a comfortable, inviting, respectful setting where everyone is seen as equal and valued.
2. Integrate intentional instructional strategies across content areas to foster the emotional, social, and academic skills that promote belonging.
3. Ensure that all students have multiple, varied chances to participate in classroom and school events and activities, express their own voices, and make choices in their learning activities.

4. Adhere to high standards for academics and behavior, with caring and appropriate support to help every student succeed and reach the standards. This expectation increases academic belonging by helping students to see themselves and peers as having equal and powerful abilities to learn and grow as students.

5. Work with colleagues and students' families to foster a school environment that embodies an authentic sense of caring and trust among the school community.

6. Consistently model beliefs, attitudes, and behaviors that promote belonging, equity, and competence for all students.

What's in This Book and How to Use It

Each chapter offers strategies, advice, dos and don'ts, and specific activities to help you create a well-managed classroom that increases student belonging. Each of the 50 strategies is grounded in two things: the conditions that advance belonging and secure, consistent management that supports optimal learning for all students.

In Chapter 1, we offer some **advice and practices to get yourself and your classroom ready for a successful school year.** Some strategies in this chapter are intended to deepen your understanding of belonging and help you reflect on how your attitudes, practices, and beliefs affect belonging and classroom management. Other strategies guide you to make plans that will set all your students on the path to belonging in the early days and weeks of school.

Chapters 2 through 7 focus on the **fundamental aspects of classroom culture and learning,** detailing strategies that will help you teach, practice, and expand the skills of relationship building; create a safe, enriching, and consistent environment; foster critical social and emotional skills; create academic learning experiences that will increase all students' mastery and competence; and help students work, grow, and learn more successfully in groups.

All the strategies in this book are designed to promote optimal classroom management and belongingness. Choose the strategies from each chapter that fit your classroom, your needs, and the needs of your students. Also bear in mind that all these categories of strategies need consistent attention throughout the year; none are as just for the beginning of the school year. Many of the strategies can be repeated—with new content or other adaptations—several times throughout the year.

We Belong is designed primarily for teachers and students in upper elementary, middle, and high school, but most of the concepts and practices are readily adaptable to lower grade levels. It is intended for teachers at all levels of experience. The strategies we describe can be useful in preservice experiences, help a new teacher get off to a great start with effective belonging-centered management, and prompt seasoned teachers to rethink and fine-tune their management to enhance belonging. Some strategies do ask you to draw upon previous teaching experience. If you've had none, save those for later, when you have a few weeks under your belt, or ask for input from colleagues.

Further, the strategies in this book (and the philosophy behind them) work in a variety of educational settings, including homeschooling environments, counseling sessions, athletic team training, student councils and other clubs, and even the principal's office. They are also useful for teacher training, team collaboration, grade-level or department improvement efforts, or professional development plans. Whatever your status as an educator, we hope you'll choose the strategies that speak to your needs, in the order that best helps you and most benefits your students.

 This icon indicates a downloadable tool. You are invited to download a free PDF of the book's collection of 18 tools (reflection activities, surveys, templates, and so on; see page viii) at **http://www.ascd.org/we-belong-122002**.

How to Fit This Work into Everything Else You're Doing

The approach to classroom management we advocate is about adjusting what you already think, believe, plan, and say, in ways that increase your students' sense of belonging and improve the climate for learning. Any effort and time you invest in increasing connection for students will have a profound effect on their overall social, emotional, and academic well-being and on how your classroom feels and functions. Time spent on belonging skills will drastically cut the time you spend on behavior management and pay off in the increased academic engagement of your students.

Throughout our many years of working with students of all grade levels (between the two of us, we have taught kindergartners through seniors), one theme has surfaced repeatedly: students have a profound need and desire to find places where they feel they belong and where they can discover who they are and who they want to become. This realization culminated in our writing of *Middle School: A Place to Belong and Become* (Barron & Kinney, 2018), but our passion for the importance of belonging did not end with that book's publication. Our research revealed striking connections between classroom management styles and the levels of belonging (or not belonging) students experience, and we were compelled to explore this connection further.

This book gives voice to that research and to what the two of us have seen and experienced in our own practice: that all students need a profusion of concrete belonging-focused experiences and skills. And they need them in the context of an inviting, comfortable, and well-managed environment where everyone is treated as equal, capable, and valuable.

When you try belonging-centered classroom management, you'll reap benefits well worth the time you spend with these strategies. You'll give your students the gift of increased social-emotional competence and the gift of a highly functional and positive learning environment—one in which they know with absolute certainty that every student is wanted and valued here. Every student can succeed here, within this community. And every student shares the same powerful conviction: *We belong.*

1

Belonging Thrives When Teachers Believe and Prepare

When I don't belong, I feel invisible and completely alone.
a 10th grader

---

*This chapter includes information, self-reflection prompts, and active strategies
to help you get ready to develop a climate and classroom management
plan where belonging can thrive. We also include some tips for designing
a first-day plan to kick off your belonging practices the right way.*

Ahh! The days of vacation break—those long weeks of summer or between school terms. You try to forget about the planning, the students' needs, the bureaucracy, the schedules, and the issues. Most teachers look forward to these times, even when the break is filled with the bustle (and sometimes pressures) of family activities, travel, graduate studies, professional development, or short-term jobs. But not too far into the "break," most teachers start thinking about the coming year, which includes thinking about classroom management and relationships with students. One teacher we know ends the year by making a list of "Things I Vow to Do Differently Next Year." On and off all summer, she gathers ideas for ways to start the year on a better foot, management-wise, and keep it consistent throughout the year.

An *Education Week* survey about the sense of belonging at school (Blad, 2017) collected responses from 528 educators. Over 80 percent of the respondents reported the personal belief that it is important for students to feel they belong in the classroom—and over 40 percent of respondents said it was very challenging for them to find strategies to help students fit in. Our own experience as educators and our contacts with educators throughout the country has led us to a similar conclusion: Teachers believe that belonging is important for student academic success and overall well-being, yet they're not always sure how to help this happen.

Belief in the importance of belonging, alone, is not enough. If your classroom is to have successful belonging-centered management at its core, you must be prepared *before* students show up with strategies that will work to promote both belonging and good classroom management. This begins with your understanding of belonging and how it is nourished (or impaired), which in turn requires exploring the elements of management that are affected by students' levels of belongingness.

Strategy 1: Reflect on Belonging

The first step in engaging with the topic of belonging and its connection to classroom management is this: *Consider what belonging means to you.* Your perspective on belonging is influenced by your own experiences and situations you've witnessed (or heard about secondhand) that involved others—such as your own children, your students, or your colleagues. Your history with belonging helps form your attitudes about it and guides the approaches you are compelled to use in addressing it for your students.

Here are some prompts to get you started:

1. Describe or define *belonging* as you understand it, based on your own experiences.
2. List a few places or situations where you feel or have felt a sense of belonging.
3. How can you "tell" you belong in those places or situations? Dig into those feelings of belongingness and describe them.
4. List a few places or situations in which you feel or have felt a *lack* of belonging.
5. Think back to your student days. What factors contributed to your sense of belonging (or not belonging) at school or in a classroom?

6. List some signs you look for or have seen that suggest students in your classroom don't feel a sense of belonging.

7. Describe what and how you feel when you see a student (or perhaps a child of your own) struggle with belonging.

8. Describe your past experiences—successes and failures—with helping students feel they belong.

9. Describe the ways in which your own background, culture, and life experiences are **similar** to those of your students.

10. Describe the ways in which your own background, culture, and life experiences are **different** from those of your students.

As the icon at the list's start indicates, this reflection activity is included in the downloadable toolset at http://www.ascd.org/we-belong-122002. As or after you respond to these prompts, think about the implications your answers might have for your teaching and classroom management. You might also complete and discuss this activity with colleagues in a grade level, team, department, or staff meeting.

Strategy 2: Boost Your Belonging IQ

Are you ready to deepen your belonging understandings and insights? Here are some questions to guide you through a reflective second reading of this book's Introduction. You may flip (or click) back through the text, highlighting and making notes on the page, or you can download a copy of these questions as a worksheet.

1. Review the opening text of the Introduction—the three paragraphs beginning on page 1. Highlight (or record) the words, phrases, or ideas that stand out to you. Make notes about why these grabbed you.

2. Highlight the definitions of *belonging* and *school belonging* in the "What Belonging Is" section, beginning on page 2. Read them aloud. Then, in this same section, highlight the final two sentences of the Baumeister and Leary quote. Read these sentences out loud. What stands out to you? What experiences from your own practice do they call to mind?

3. Review the list of the research-verified benefits of belonging in the section "Why Belonging in School Matters," beginning on page 3. Highlight

any benefits you have personally witnessed. What other characteristics or benefits of belonging you have seen?

4. On pages 3–4, review the bulleted list of what students can experience when they do not feel a sense of belonging in school. Highlight consequences you have personally witnessed. What other consequences of "not belonging" have you seen?

5. In the "How to Increase Belongingness" section (beginning on p. 4), put a checkmark by factors you already attend to. Circle or highlight factors that challenge you, that you haven't thought much about, that you would like to learn more about, or that you would like to increase your abilities to provide.

6. Review the section titled "Classroom Management—and the Difference It Makes" (beginning on p. 5). Carefully reread the final two paragraphs. In your own words, briefly summarize the partnership between classroom management and belonging.

7. In that same section, highlight concepts or messages about classroom management that excite you. Which do you find most compelling?

8. In the section, "How to Combine Belonging and Management in Practice" (beginning on p. 8), highlight the topic sentence or key idea in the opening paragraph.

9. In that same section, reread each of the six actions for increasing belonging. Pause after each one and ask yourself, "Can I commit to doing this consistently and better than I have already been doing?" Jot down one idea or goal for action next to each of the six actions.

10. What one sentence, phrase, or idea from the Introduction was the most powerful or memorable to you? Write it down. Continue to refer to it as you make your way through the book.

Strategy 3: Celebrate Successful Belonging Practices

Most likely, many techniques and activities that you currently use *do* help students feel they belong. You just might not have been aware that these were belonging-promoting practices.

For example, when Patti was a teacher, she often started the day with five to seven minutes of no-pressure sharing time. She might relate something that happened to her the night before or ask the students a question such as "What's happened in your life since I saw you yesterday?" It definitely added a family feeling to the classroom, and she found it especially heartwarming when a fairly shy student would volunteer a story.

Figure 1.1's brainstorming guide can prompt you to review what you're doing now and consider the scope of your practice and categories your actions might fall into. What are some of your current practices that further belonging in your classroom? List them by category or download a copy of the brainstorming guide and record them in the space provided. Celebrate your belonging practices and find ways to strengthen and expand them.

FIGURE 1.1

Brainstorming Guide: What You Already Do to Help Students Belong

Attitudes, beliefs, and behaviors you model	Ways you relate to students	Expectations you communicate to students
Activities that intentionally teach emotional skills	Activities that intentionally teach social skills	Activities that boost students' confidence in themselves as learners
Activities that help students see one another's strengths and value	Activities that give students opportunity to express their opinions	Activities that give students opportunity to make choices about their own learning

Strategy 4: Examine Management Practices That Affect Belonging

A major premise of this book is *the way a teacher manages a classroom strongly affects whether or not students feel that they belong.* Management protocols or procedures, even those that seem minor, can either bolster or sabotage progress toward belongingness.

So now that you're thinking about belonging, it's a good time to do a checkup on your own classroom management practices and set some goals for increasing belongingness. Use the procedure mapped out in Figure 1.2.

FIGURE 1.2

Reflection: Does Your Classroom Management Enhance Belonging?

Part I. Examine your classroom management in light of the need for students to belong.

A. List 8 of your management practices or strategies.

(Think about classroom setting, schedule, organization, classroom protocols and procedures, relationships with students, expectations and consequences, problem resolution, your responses to misbehavior, style of instruction, etc.)

B. Go back and thoughtfully examine each one you listed with a focus on belonging. Ask, "Does this help students belong?" Write YES! or Keep! or write NO! or Improve! (for cases where your approach could impede belonging or set it back). Remember: All students are different, and just because something makes one student feel as if he belongs, it may not make someone else feel as if she belongs. For example, recognizing a student accomplishment may make one student feel proud and another student feel embarrassed.

Part II. Identify areas for improvement. Start planning new or changed practices and record this information in the chart space provided or in a similar format.

A. Identify four items from your list that have a NO! label. For each one, set a goal to work toward right away. Name the category for the goal (relationships, consequences, communication, protocols, etc.).

B. Write each goal in specific terms of what you will do that is a new or changed practice. It should be a goal that can be measured. (Ask yourself, "How will I know when this goal has been met?")

C. Set a date for checking up on yourself. Once school is in session, mark goals you are meeting. For others, make a plan of next steps, practices, or adjustments for making better progress. Consider doing this strategy in collaboration with a colleague.

Category	Goal	Checkup Date

Strategy 5: Include Families in School Belonging

When students see that their family and community are welcomed, comfortable, and involved in the school and classroom, their own sense of belonging takes a leap. When you are welcoming to students' families and invite their input, you build a relationship that will serve as a major support for your students' well-being and school success and a foundation for positive and effective classroom management.

The first step in forging family and community connections is to open the lines of communication. Think about how and when you will communicate with families, how and when they can contact you, and how to help them be comfortable with these communications. A one-size-fits-all communication plan probably won't cut it—especially if your student body is culturally and socioeconomically diverse. Email may work for some, phone calls for others, and face-to-face may be your best option with a few. Establish which communication methods each family prefers, the best times to reach them, and any translation that might be needed so you can begin effective communication right away. Here are some approaches we recommend.

Letter Exchange—From Teacher to Family

Start the process of family and community belonging before school begins or within the first few days of school. Write a letter that you mail or email to the family of every student—yes, even if you teach middle and high schoolers. In your personalized letter,

- Identify yourself. "Hello! I'm [your name], soon to be [student's name]'s [grade level or subject] teacher."
- Welcome the student and the family to the school and express how pleased you are to have that student in your class.
- Share your passion for the work you do. Offer a taste of what will happen in the first few weeks (something the students will study, or learn, or be able to do) and some of your goals for the year.
- Invite the family to contact you with any questions or comments; ask them to let you know the best time and way for you to contact them. Provide a variety of ways for them to contact you, including (at your discretion) by email, text, phone, and sending in or dropping off a note at the school.

Keep your letter upbeat and warm, with an obvious spirit of inclusion. Your letter should be error-free (have a friend or colleague proofread it for you); written in clear, easy-to-understand language; and translated into the family's language, if needed (a guidance counselor or teachers a student has had before can be helpful in sharing language requirements guidance if you are writing before the school year starts). It can be beneficial to draft your letter and then put it aside for a day before rereading it. As you write and as you read, ask yourself, "Will this set the belonging tone for this student's family and community?"

Letter Exchange—Home to Teacher

In your letter to parents or guardians (or via a follow-up email or text), give them an "assignment": to write you a letter telling you about their child. Suggest something along the lines of "Tell me about your child in a million words or less."

When Laurie's daughter Emma was a junior in high school, she brought home "parent homework" from her precalculus teacher on the first day of school. Laurie was asked to share things about Emma, such as problems she may experience; her strengths and weaknesses; past school experiences; and Laurie's expectations of the class, the teacher, and her daughter. Laurie found that she spent way more time than she initially thought she would on this "homework." She enjoyed sharing about Emma and found herself really pleased that the teacher had given her this opportunity. There were no "points" given to Emma for Laurie's completion or lack thereof, which made it feel like a safe assignment. The teacher also followed up with Laurie individually and addressed many of the things Laurie had shared, which made Laurie feel instantly more connected and more open to communicating with the teacher (something we sometimes lose as our children get older).

If you have a large number of students, "a million words or less" about each one might seem daunting. If so, you might ask parents for a short note, an email, or a single text to tell you something they'd like you to know about their child's strengths, interests, or needs. Tailor the assignment to your particular class and age group. Encourage families who speak a language other than English to write you in the language they're most comfortable using. Any challenge of translating these communications will be well worth the message that your classroom—their classroom, too—is a place where all students (and their families) are accepted and belong.

A gentle reminder: Be careful not to unintentionally embarrass or single out students whose family does not participate in a home-to-teacher letter exchange.

Strategy 6: Cultivate Belonging from Day 1

We remember a time when beginning teachers were cautioned, "Don't smile until Christmas." The underlying message—to be strict and never too friendly—was seemingly based on the old adage "If you give kids an inch, they'll take a mile." Implied here was that once your students were trained to conform to expectations, just maybe, by the holiday break, you could loosen up enough to be your smiling and occasionally joke-cracking human self around them.

Neither one of us took well to this advice. From the beginning, it felt more natural to let all of our students know that our classrooms—*their* classrooms— were places where students could feel safe, respected, and cared for. To be clear: *friendly* doesn't mean lax, and *collaboration* doesn't mean chaos. Our classrooms were structured without being confining, organized without being rigid; we set high expectations without using fear as a motivator.

The first day of school is your first step on the road to a classroom where students can feel they belong. It's your first chance to express to students what your class will be like—what will happen, what they can expect, what's valued, how they'll be treated, what you believe and feel about students, and what relationships in the classroom might be like. All of these messages—when positive, hopeful, and respectful—can contribute to smoother classroom management and a space where belonging thrives.

Here's a goal for Day 1: no matter what grade level or how many classes you teach, *every student* will leave your classroom feeling and least starting to believe the following:

- I'm going to be safe here.
- We're going to be serious about learning, treating one another well, and getting along. Everyone here matters equally.
- Learning is going to be active and creative. We're going to work together as well as on our own.
- I can be academically successful here.
- We're going to be heard. My ideas, interests, and experiences matter.
- I'm going to belong here.
- I want to come back.

Day 1 Checklist

How does one achieve this lofty goal? By making sure the first day or first class includes events that concretely demonstrate the truth or possibility of each of these statements.

The checklist in Figure 1.3 includes specific, observable actions and experiences—involving aspects of climate, relationships, and engagement—that will nurture belonging and spark students' overall interest in meaningful participation. You can provide the experiences chosen from the checklist through a variety of activities, lessons, or minilessons.

FIGURE 1.3

Day 1 Checklist

My Day 1 Goals

☐ Greet each student at the door.

☐ Show that I know their names or am making an effort to do so.

☐ Demonstrate that I value everyone and that I'm glad each one of them is in my classroom.

☐ Show that I am excited about my job.

☐ Share something about myself.

☐ Learn something about each student—and help them learn things about one another.

☐ Establish one routine.

☐ Have students solve a problem in pairs or small groups.

☐ Have students create or produce a piece of artwork together.

☐ Have students do something academic that is active, relevant, and meaningful— and in which they can experience success.

☐ Provide student choice in some aspect of learning.

☐ Express and share the understanding that school, and our classroom, is a safe place.

☐ Ensure my students have a memorable ending to the class or day.

Day 1 Plan

The template in Figure 1.4 can help you rough out a plan for a first day of school that emphasizes a spirit of enthusiasm, learning, and belonging. You might address some or all of your chosen outcomes from the checklist within a single lesson or activity or pursue them in one main activity plus some other brief

FIGURE 1.4

Template for Planning Day 1

Directions: Note a strategy, idea of things to say, or activity for each of these first-day components. Some strategies may satisfy more than one category.

How I will greet my students:	
How I will learn my students' names:	
What I want to share about myself and how I will do that:	
How my students will learn about one another:	
How I will assure my students of their value and safety:	
Routine(s) I will establish:	
Collaborative small-group learning activity I will provide:	
Academic activity or lesson that includes ☐ Something to read: ☐ Something to create: ☐ Something fun: ☐ Opportunity for student voice: ☐ Opportunity for student choice: ☐ An academic success for all: ☐ Reference to/use of something in the classroom: ☐ Lesson/activity description:	
How I will end class memorably:	

exchanges. To incorporate more of the experiences, extend your plan over the first two or three class periods or days.

Strategy 7: Take Care of Yourself

Teaching is a demanding, high-expectation profession. If you're like most teachers we know, you tend to think about your students first: ways to connect with them, plan lessons they will find engaging and effective, and meet their needs no matter what those needs are. You've also probably experienced the downside of this commitment—the kind of tiredness and burnout that can lead you to be less patient, speak more sharply than you mean to, or just feel somewhat out of control. In the midst of taking on so much and trying to do it all well, teachers often do an insufficient job of attending to their own needs. Raise your hand if you don't always eat right, exercise enough, get sufficient sleep, spend quality time with families and friends, or do all the things you really enjoy, which help you relax, refresh, and reenergize.

Make clear, deliberate choices that contribute to your own emotional and physical health—so that you can both be at your best and model attention to well-being for your students. Before you get into your first few whirlwind weeks of school, take a pause (and a deep breath) to sketch out some plans for self-care. Schedule the positive practices or habits you'll attend to during the school day and outside school.

Here are some ideas we've collected from colleagues and used ourselves.

During the school day . . .

- Don't forget to breathe! Sometimes all it takes is to stop what you're doing or saying, pause, and take a nice, deep breath and slowly release it (a good technique to teach your students, too).
- Eat some protein—nuts, cheese, or a granola bar.
- Drink a glass of water.
- Squeeze a stress ball.
- Read a thank-you note. (It's good to keep a file of positive notes to pull out in times of need.)
- Read a positive quote. (Again, keep a folder of quotes that you like.)
- Get a little exercise! Walk quickly up and down the hall. Hop from side to side for 60 seconds. Treat your room like an obstacle course and walk around it 10 times.
- If you have a short break, go outside for a few minutes. Yes, you can walk, but fresh air and sunshine have independent benefits.
- Reach out to students' parents with a call or email or send a postcard with some positive news. (This can really work wonders on a difficult day.)
- Listen to some favorite music between classes. Sing along!
- Close your eyes for a few minutes. (Set an alarm in case you fall asleep!)

Outside school . . .

- **Move.** Run, walk, ski, dance, bike, hike, paddle, golf, do yoga, lift weights, do CrossFit—do whatever you enjoy that gets you moving. Do it with your family and friends, adding the benefit of healthy, quality time with those you love.
- **Relax.** Read a fun book, schedule in "do-nothing" time, watch a favorite TV show, take a hot bath or long shower, chat with a best friend, go for a scenic drive, go to bed earlier than usual, listen to music, get a massage, spend time alone, meditate.

- **Pursue a hobby.** Read, play an instrument, bake, cook, sew, knit, build, craft, garden, paint, upcycle, take photos, join a podcast or a book club.
- **Volunteer.** Offer your services at an animal shelter, a soup kitchen or food pantry, a national park or local hospital, a library or museum, or the American Red Cross. Visit a nursing home and talk to or play music for residents. Sign on to a Habitat for Humanity project.

We love sharing this quote by author L. R. Knost: "Taking care of yourself doesn't mean me first, it means me too" (2017). Build into your schedule some things that make you feel good, refresh your spirit, and keep you going. Yes, it will take some time, but don't feel guilty about taking that time. Your mental health depends on it. Your students will thank you, your family will thank you, and your body will thank you, as well.

2

Belonging Thrives on Trusting Relationships

When I am welcomed and involved, I belong.

A 5th grader

This chapter highlights teacher behaviors and attitudes that begin and deepen secure, meaningful relationships with students. The strategies will help you and your students get to know one another, build class cohesiveness and pride, and establish the sense that every student is an equal, valued, and contributing part of the group. You'll find some tactics for nurturing quality peer relationships, using humor to enhance relationships, being attentive to how individuals are faring, and further strengthening bonds with your students' families. These strategies set the stage for classroom processes that define and practice values such as respect, kindness, acceptance, and inclusion. They help to deepen belonging as well as to diminish behavior issues.

Relationships are at the heart of every classroom. Once the school year begins and students flood your classroom, you're automatically swept into anywhere from 30 to 130 new relationships. You and your students are also surrounded by—enmeshed in—a myriad of other relationships developed with one another. Add on numerous relationships with students' parents and families. All of these connections (and disconnections) influence what goes on in your classroom.

The relationship that teachers form with their students is generally understood to be very powerful; it is a crucial component in furthering (or deterring) belonging and, thus, a key determinant in the success (or downfall) of classroom management. A supportive relationship with one or more teachers is the strongest predictor of school belonging for an individual student (Allen et al., 2016). And the dynamics of classroom management procedures are rooted in the kinds of relationships students have with their teachers (Pianta, 1999).

There is an extensive research base to support the conclusion that caring and trusting relationships are essential for learning (Alexander, Entwisle, & Horsey, 1997; Baker, Grant, & Morlock, 2008; Birch & Ladd, 1998; Bryk & Schneider, 2002; Decker, Dona, & Christenson, 2007; Elledge, Elledge, Newgent, & Cavell, 2016; Hamre & Pianta, 2001; Huang, Lewis, Cohen, Prewett, & Herman, 2018; Konishi, Hymal, Zumbo, & Zhen, 2010; Konishi & Wong, 2018; Marzano, Marzano, & Pickering, 2003; O'Connor, Dearing, & Collins, 2011; Silver, Measelle, Armstrong, & Essex, 2005). We know, for example, that strong teacher–student relationships

- Improve students' academic performance.
- Reduce behavior problems in the classroom.
- Positively affect students' treatment of one another.
- Provide a foundation for successful academic and behavioral interventions.
- Improve students' self-esteem and self-regulation.
- Increase student engagement.
- Heighten student motivation and self-direction.
- Help students feel secure.
- Encourage student cooperation.
- Supply a buffering effect in the presence of bullying.

Murray and Malmgren (2005) assert that positive relationships with teachers are particularly beneficial for students facing the risks associated with poverty. Their study demonstrated students from low-income families who have strong relationships with their teachers have better social-emotional adjustment and greater academic gains than peers without such relationships. We believe this concept can be extended to other marginalized groups. Students of color, students with physical and cognitive differences, LGBTQ students, students who are recent immigrants, and students struggling with mental health challenges will also benefit from the power of a strong relationship with a trusting and trusted teacher.

Peer relationships play powerful roles for every student, every day, in every class. As with teacher–student relationships, peer contacts are a major factor in school well-being and success (or lack thereof). Although this is true for all students at all grade levels, these relationships have increasing influence at the middle and high school levels (Li, Lynch, Kalvin, Liu, & Lerner, 2011; Steinberg & Monahan, 2007).

Positive or satisfying peer relationships have been found to contribute positively to academic success, prosocial behavior, engagement, self-confidence and self-belief, self-management, school satisfaction and enjoyment, and sense of belonging (Hu, 2008; Li et al., 2011; Roffey, 2012; Rohrbeck & Gray, 2014; Wentzel & Caldwell, 1997). In contrast, negative or nonexistent social contacts that exclude, reject, demean, bully, or discriminate based on race, ethnicity, sexual orientation, religion, or social group have negative (sometimes devastating) effects on students. Such relationships present serious impediments to any kind of satisfaction or success at school, with such outcomes as self-doubt, anxiety, declining academic performance, and antisocial behavior (Elledge et al., 2016; Hu, 2008; Kemple & Hartle, 1997; Li et al., 2011; Rohrbeck & Gray, 2014; Wentzel & Caldwell, 1997).

Sparking trust and connection with and among students is just the beginning. The strategies you use early in the year begin relationships that can develop over time, through ongoing, genuine interest in your students' lives, regular and meaningful interactions, active watching and listening, and mutual respect. You'll find that this relationship-building process fuels gains in belonging and naturally leads to more positive behavior in the classroom.

And when it comes to classroom management, the trust you accrue with students is like money in the bank. Strong communication with and understanding of individual students serve you well for difficulties that may arise later on. When times get rough, you can draw on those deposits of goodwill to help solve problems.

Strategy 8: Build Belonging with Relationship Promises

You'll spend the entire school year relating to students, and every day you'll get to know more about them. During the first few days and weeks of school, however, students will form their strongest impressions about how you perceive them, care about them, and relate to them. A teacher only gets one chance to start a new relationship with a student.

Put just as much effort into thinking about the relationships you'll establish and promote in your classroom as you expend on the content you'll teach. Facing all those new relationships will be less intimidating if you're prepared when the bell rings on that first day. Because relationships are at the heart of every classroom, they're also at the heart of effective classroom management.

What does a caring, trusting teacher–student relationship look like in practice? Figure 2.1 points you to a good starting place: 25 promises you can make for

---

FIGURE 2.1

25 Promises to Make to Students

Directions: Preface each promise with "I will . . . ," and say them out loud to yourself. Highlight those that you do consistently. Set goals to increase your consistency on the others. Review the promises and repeat this process at least once a month.

1   Provide a structured (not rigid), predictable, and safe environment.

2   Be agreeable, be patient, smile, encourage constantly, and speak kindly.

3   Treat all students with respect at all times.

4   Be fair—while realizing "fair" may not always be "equal" for each student.

5   Give messages of equal worth for all students; show no biases or favoritism.

6   Be trustworthy, keep my word, and do what I say I will do.

7   Keep students safe from taunting, derision, discrimination, exclusion, and bullying of any kind.

8   Set procedures and expectations and follow through on them—consistently.

9   Show passion for the subject and concepts I teach and show students that I enjoy teaching them.

10   Set clear expectations for students to treat one another respectfully, teach them explicitly what that means, and hold them to expectations equitably.

11   Set high learning expectations and help my students meet them; help them over individual learning hurdles, and let all students know that I believe they can succeed.

12   Learn constantly about students as a group and as individuals.

13   Honor each student's unique qualities, abilities, and interests.

14   Give students stress-free, embarrassment-free ways to communicate with me.

15   Confront students' misbehavior in private, never disciplining anyone in front of others.

16   Make some positive contact with each student every day.

17   Ask for and listen to students' opinions, ideas, and evaluations; act on them.

18   Laugh, embrace and include humor, and show that I enjoy being with students.

19   Be available for each student and all students.

20   Never yell, threaten, manipulate, shame, ridicule, label, judge, or demean.

21   Make my nonverbal messages as caring and nonthreatening as my words.

22   Be an obvious and passionate advocate for each student.

23   Let students see evidence that I am helping every one of them belong.

24   Be honest, direct, and real.

25   Make learning fun.

your relationship with your students. All of the "promises" are actions that your students can witness daily. Examine these closely, review them regularly, and treat them as promises to yourself, too. Think about which of these actions you already take and how you can be more consistent with them. Think about which of these promises you're willing to make for the first time and create a plan, with goals and timelines, for yourself to follow. In addition to kicking off solid relationships with your students, these behaviors on their own will increase belonging and make students feel safer. Notice, too, that all of these actions are also attributes of good classroom management.

Strategy 9: Seek a Relationship Lesson from Your Students

The best guidance you'll find on building trusting teacher–student relationships won't come from research, from books, or even from colleagues; it will come from your students themselves. You just need to ask them. And then you need to act on what they tell you and keep asking.

Step 1: Survey Your Students

How will you invite your students to help you learn about them and what they need from you? One way is to give them some time to think about teacher–student relationships and answer some questions about the topic. Figure 2.2 provides a sample survey that you can adapt for your students' level and your classroom. Choose and word questions appropriately for your grade level. Offer a moderate number of questions and provide some choice. For example, explain that they don't necessarily have to answer all questions, or invite them to write and respond to their own questions. It's a good idea to wait a few weeks after school has started for a survey effort like this—after you've already learned enough about your students to customize the survey appropriately.

Most students will probably feel safest responding privately, with no name attached to written responses or with names optional. Or you might find that a survey works well in pairs, where students can bounce ideas off one another before responding.

FIGURE 2.2

Student Survey on Teacher–Student Relationships

Instructions: Answer as many as of these questions as you can. Don't include your name or any student or teacher names.

Part 1

1. How can you tell that a teacher accepts or values you?

2. What teacher actions make you wonder whether the teacher likes you or not?

3. What helps you trust a teacher?

4. What makes it hard to trust a teacher?

5. What is the best action you've seen a teacher do in relating to students?

6. What helps you feel positive about a teacher?

7. What causes you to feel uncomfortable with a teacher?

8. What do you wish teachers would do *for sure*?

9. What do you wish teachers would NOT do *for sure*?

Part 2

1. Do you think your teacher(s) would notice if you are having trouble with something you are learning?

2. Do you think your teacher(s) would notice if you are upset about something going on at school?

3. How can you tell when a teacher is really interested in you?

4. How can you tell when a teacher is determined to help you succeed in school?

Part 3

What are one or two top pieces of advice you'd give a teacher about what students your age need?

How will you introduce the survey? No matter how you say it, the message you want to convey to students is that you want to learn about teacher–student relationships *from them*. Be sure to stress the privacy aspect. Explain that just as you are committing to keep the information they share private, they shouldn't name other students or teachers—although you are open to them addressing *your* habits. You might say something like this:

> You've all been in school long enough to have contacts and connections with several teachers. The way a teacher relates to you makes a difference in how safe, comfortable, and supported you feel. It also makes a difference in how well you learn. I'd like you to think about what teachers do, have done, or could do to have relationships that make it possible for students to trust and feel safe

with them. Your ideas will help me learn how to develop the best possible relationships with you. I'd like you to give some careful thought to these questions.
You don't have to answer them all. I just ask that you answer at least three questions in the first part and at least two in the second part. I'd really like you to
answer the final question, though.

You will be amazed at what you learn from just asking. Even elementary students
can give you useful feedback.

Step 2: Use What You Learn

Once you have asked for students' advice, create a list of things you will do to make
use of what they've told you. Set specific goals. Tell students what you learned and
what you'll be working on. If you share your list and your goals with them, they
will see that you have listened and that you take their input seriously.

By the way, just doing an activity like this one boosts your relationships with
your students. It lets them know you value them, want their input, and respect
their experience and ideas. Your response to their responses can deepen their
trust and strengthen relationships even further.

Step 3: Repeat the Process

Keep learning from students throughout the school year. When they seem comfortable with the survey process, you can ask more specifically about *your* actions
in the ways you relate to them. For example, both of us have used versions of this
shorter survey:

1. What should I keep doing?
2. What should I stop doing?
3. What should I start doing?
4. Do you believe I like you?
5. Anything else I need to know or that you want to tell me?

You might also invite students to create their version of this survey—perhaps one
with statements to which they respond according to a rating scale (e.g., *always,
often, some of the time, not often, never*). The questions they choose are themselves
valuable formative data for your ongoing relationship work.

Strategy 10: Get to Know Your Students

Few pieces of advice are more important to hear and follow than this: Get to know your students. Some of this means building an expert understanding of the developmental characteristics of the age group you teach, but it also means staying abreast of current expressions or memes, trends, habits, fashion, and so on. More important still, it means learning about each of your students *as an individual*. What is his background? What languages does her family speak at home? What's her family history and culture? What talents does he have? Where has he struggled? Being able to answer questions like these strengthens your efforts to build relationships with students and alerts you to additional resources that may enhance your teaching. This "getting to know each" process lays the groundwork for positive classroom management strategies and healthy, satisfying classroom relationships.

Unfortunately, many classroom management approaches are based on the premise that all students need the same kind of relationship with the teacher. This is a lesson Patti learned painfully early in her teaching career. She had a student named John who was challenging and needed constant reminding and redirecting in order to stay on task. One day, he actually completed all the assigned tasks without a reminder, and Patti drew attention to this by complimenting him in front of the class. It was a long time before John repeated this achievement. Another student, David, was quiet and shy. He struggled to spell correctly and write clearly, but while deciphering the descriptions he came up with, Patti found that they were vivid and compelling. Impressed, she shared with the class something David had written. David seldom inserted such phrases in his writing after that. In both cases, Patti had wrongly assumed that public recognition of good work habits and good work would be a positive reward. For these two boys, it wasn't.

Here are some ways to learn about the likes and dislikes, hopes, worries, preferences, and school experiences of students. Start these practices early in the school year. Repeat them as appropriate—some regularly, some occasionally.

Meet and Greet

Learn your students' names as quickly as you can. Welcome them at the door, every day, by name. This type of small interaction with you each day has huge benefits:

- You establish and demonstrate the understanding that "This is our class, and we are in this together."
- You show that you care about that student, which leads to the development of relationships that last far beyond a greeting at the door.
- You get an immediate "read" on each student's mood and state of mind and notice who's showing signs of belonging or not belonging.
- You can tell who looks eager, tired, withdrawn, or stressed; this is your chance to bring a ray of light into a day that might be going poorly.

With a pat on the shoulder, a genuine smile, or a friendly comment, you can (sometimes unknowingly) head off potential classroom disruptions before they ever begin. If you "read" an eager, enthusiastic, or positive frame of mind, you have a chance to affirm that and help it continue.

As students enter or leave the room, resist the urge to complete a quick task at your desk, chat with a colleague, or work on setting up something for the next class. Do your best to have those logistical tasks handled before the day or class begins.

End the day or the class period the same way. Be at the door as students leave. Make sure that each student hears you say goodbye or some other fun send-off phrase. Don't let anyone leave unnoticed or unencouraged.

Finish-the-Thought Messages

Unfinished statements can spark ideas, memories, and opinions—and they offer an easy way for your students to share something about themselves. Choose topics that will give you a glimpse into students' self-view, personal skills, and interests or that let you know something about how they see themselves as students or about their experiences with and attitudes about school. Here are some ideas for statements students can finish:

I'm good at/I'd like to get better at . . .
People like me because . . .
I really like it when a teacher . . .
I don't like it when a teacher . . .
My best experience in school has been . . .
My most unpleasant experience in school has been . . .
I'd like to learn how to . . .

What I hope will happen this year at school (or in this class) is . . .

What I hope *doesn't* happen this year at school is . . .

I really like/dislike [a particular subject] because . . .

One way you can help me do my best in class is . . .

Something that's important for you to know about me is . . .

The best thing about me is . . .

I struggle with . . .

I worry about . . .

I am happiest when I am . . .

I feel the best about myself when I am . . .

There are many ways to present this activity; here are a few ideas:

- Put a list of starting phrases on the board or forward the list to students' devices; ask students to choose three to five phrases to finish.
- Use one as an "exit ticket." In the last five minutes of class, give students a half-sheet of paper and ask them to put their names at the top and complete a specific starter. Collect them as students are dismissed.
- Give each student a handout with some sentence starters to complete over several days. Ask them to write their names on the paper, assign a specific number of starters (so they have a choice), and collect them before they leave class. Return the papers the next day(s) for them to complete a few more.
- Ask students to use the prompts as food for thought for a letter or email to you. Tell them you want to learn what motivates them in school, how they learn best, what they hope to learn from you, what makes them angry, what helps them feel comfortable, or anything else they want you to know. (If using email, be sure to diligently follow school protocols for communicating electronically with students. Most schools require a professional, closed platform for communications, meaning you shouldn't use your personal accounts.)

As you can see, it's important to provide several response options rather than risk overwhelming students with too many questions at once. Even with older students, you'll get more thoughtful responses if you request a manageable number (just as with the student survey in Strategy 9). Keep a confidential file with these papers and any other written communications from students. Take time to read (and reread) them and use what you learn to build your relationships with individual students.

Meet One-on-One

Another way to build relationships is to meet with each student one-on-one. If possible, meet with students in person. If it's not possible to meet in person, or if a virtual meeting is preferred or required and students have access, use Google Meet, Zoom, or another platform. A phone call can also work well. (Again, for any virtual contact, make sure you follow school protocols and get approval from students' families to meet with them this way.)

When COVID-19 struck in the spring of 2020 and schools across the United States transitioned to remote learning with no warning, no preparation, and no guidelines, Laurie honestly wasn't sure what advice to give teachers on maintaining relationships with students (and one another). She certainly didn't feel prepared to lead an entire school district through a global pandemic. One conversation Laurie had with an elementary school teacher has stuck with her. The teacher noted that, although it may seem that elementary teachers have the best opportunity to build deep, meaningful relationships with students because they spend so many hours every day with the same group, she had never realized how much she *didn't* know about her students until remote learning. This teacher learned so much more about each student as she spent time with them virtually—time she was never afforded in a traditional, face-to-face classroom. She learned about students' pets, hobbies, siblings, favorite games and foods, fears and hopes, worries and dreams. In the midst of some of the most difficult teaching she would ever face, she had decided that even once school resumed in person, she would always try to continue individual virtual meetings because they gave her opportunities to build relationships with students in a way she never had before.

Strategy 11: Let Students Get to Know You

When she was a teacher, Patti occasionally encountered her young students at the grocery store; they pretty much went into shock seeing her outside school. She also remembers a 5th grader whose mouth dropped open when the principal stopped by Patti's classroom to hand her a paycheck. "You mean they *pay* you for this?" he asked. During her principal years, Patti was the accompanist for the middle school choir. A 6th grader once asked her, "Are you the same Mrs. Kinney who played the piano at the concert last night?" His response when she said yes was a big, wide-eyed "Wow!"

When Laurie was a principal, one of her 6th grade math teachers just had a way of connecting with students. He could joke around and not let it go too far. He could share personal stories and not cross professional boundaries. He even could pull off wearing a *Napoleon Dynamite* T-shirt ("Vote for Pedro"). The truth was, he wasn't actually a big fan of *Napoleon Dynamite*, but he *was* a big fan of his students and a big fan of them learning math. The connections he made with them when he wore a silly shirt or showed up at their club baseball games paid great dividends in his relationships with them, his classroom management, and their subsequent math achievement.

Students of all ages (even adolescents, though they'll sometimes try not to show it) get a kick out of learning about their teachers and seeing them as real people with feelings and lives outside school. Let them know that you have interests, connections, passions, and a sense of humor. Their comfort and trust increase when you show them that there is more to you than your work.

Early in the year, create a display or project pictures of yourself when you were their age—and talk about your experiences. How did you dress? What did you do for fun? What music did you like? What popular fads did you follow? What was going on in the world then? Let them in on some of the hopes, dreams, fears, and failures you had growing up:

- Tell them what you were like as a student.
- Tell them what you thought about the subject you're teaching them.
- Share a positive experience you had with a teacher and how it influenced you.
- Tell them about something you did that was really stupid (but funny in retrospect).

You can also tell them about interesting or funny things going on right now in your life. For example:

- Thinking about getting a new car? Ask their advice!
- Did you get a new pet? Bring a picture and share your new-pet parenting ups and downs.
- Ask their thoughts on a good movie, place to eat, TV show, or video game—or share yours.

- Have a success (or failure) in the kitchen? Take and share a picture of it.
- Share a funny (age-appropriate) joke.

As you get to know students and let them get to know you, take care to be authentic. Students of all ages are good at recognizing an insincere or phony adult. Your interest in students must be real. Your joy in seeing each student each day must be sincere. The stories you tell about yourself must be true. When you laugh with them, the laughter should be real. One of the most important messages adults give to students is to be themselves and value themselves. Don't pretend to be someone you're not.

Strategy 12: Help Students Get to Know One Another

Laurie remembers a day when her 12th grade AP English class was getting ready to discuss a literary work, and a student named Bill exclaimed, "We talked about that book our in English class last year!" A student named Melanie added, "So did we! It was interesting." Bill then turned to Melanie and said, "Uh, yeah, we were in the same class. I sat right behind you." Laurie wonders to this day how one class-mate could have been invisible to another like that . . . and what effect this must have had on Bill's sense of belonging.

For students to belong and a class to operate as a community, everybody needs to know one another . . . not just be acquainted with, but really *know*. Remember, every student needs "ongoing, positive, comfortable bonds that are stable and that the student has reason to believe will continue" (Baumeister & Leary, 1995, p. 50). Melanie might actually have been *acquainted* with Bill in 11th grade English, but obviously the bond was not there. To increase students' sense of belonging, you need to plan for the kinds of interaction that sow the roots of real bonds.

During the first few weeks of school, plan specific activities that help students learn about one another. (Yes, this kind of activity is still important to do in high school.) While this will require diverting time away from content instruction, what you're banking on is that the human connections your students will develop and the attitudes of respect they internalize will set everyone up for better learn-ing down the road. Distractions and disruptions tend to diminish as students become more accepting and understanding of one another. Any time lost, you'll gain back.

Look for activities in which students will learn something memorable about one another by asking and answering questions. Try to choose options that will be as fun and as comfortable for everyone as possible. Strategy 10 (see p. 33) describes students who might withdraw when the spotlight or class attention focuses on them. Bear in mind that what seems to you like a simple icebreaker may feel threatening for a student who feels like an outsider, socially or culturally. With that said, let's look at some options.

Student-to-Student Introductions

Join students in pairs and ask them to learn two important things about each other; they will be responsible for introducing their partner to a larger group. Then, join three pairs together and give them a few minutes for the introductions. Next, ask students go back to their original pairs and learn one or two more things about each other. Repeat, but this time, join three different pairs together in the introduction process.

At the end of this exercise, no student will have been introduced to the entire class. If your class is together all day, there may be time to continue the process until all students "meet" all others. With shorter class periods, the activity can be continued on a second day. If the activity continues, keep the original pairs together so that they can continue to engage with and learn more about each other.

Icebreakers

Icebreakers are intended to stir up fun and movement and give students glimpses of one another's interests, characteristics, and personalities. Figure 2.3 lists some activities you might want to try.

Because these types of activities are generally brief, students might quickly forget what they learn about one another. Your goal is to begin to build lasting bonds, so be sure to take advantage of the sparks of knowledge icebreakers ignite. At the end of each week (or at other intervals), have students draw cards from a hat; each card should show the name of a student in the class. Ask students to talk or write about something they remember learning about the person whose name is on their card.

Although particularly well suited for the beginning of the year (which is when they are most often used), icebreaker activities are valuable throughout the year. The need for comfortable peer relationships never ends. Revisit such

FIGURE 2.3	
Activities to Help Students Learn About (and with) One Another	
Activity	**How It Works**
Signature Bingo	Create a set of Bingo-style cards (a grid of nine squares). Mark the center as a free space. Put a short description on the other spaces (e.g., has a pet dog, has a pet that is not a dog or cat, has untied shoelaces, is the oldest in the family, can name three rappers in 10 seconds, has a sibling in the same school). The task is to get a signature from a student who fits that descriptionon as many spaces as possible within a given time.
Question circles	Divide students into two groups, and make an inner and outer circle with students facing one another. Ask students a question to discuss with the person they are facing (e.g., "What's a place you never want to visit?"). Direct one of the circles to move X number of people to the right (or left) and ask a different "getting acquainted" question.
	Later in the year, this also works well to review content material. Ask a question and give students a specific amount of time to discuss and agree on an answer.
Beach ball questions	Write short "getting to know you" questions all over a large beach ball. Have students stand in a large circle and play catch with the ball. Whoever catches it must answer the question under his or her left thumb. After answering, the person tosses the ball to someone who has not held it. Be sure to join the circle. (This also works well with content questions.) Use the activity again and again to review vocabulary word meanings, spelling, math facts, or any other content.
Inventive lineups	See how fast your class can get into an alphabetical line based on their first names. Other options: line up tallest to smallest, oldest to youngest, by birthdays (January to December). You can make this more challenging by asking students to do it silently or using only hand signals to communicate.

tasks to keep your students learning about one another; as noted in Figure 2.3, you can also incorporate academic content into an activity to strengthen skills and knowledge. Find ways to keep students learning more about their classmates, relying on one another more, being productive together, and relating meaningfully every day.

Smart Seat Assignments

Deliberate seating arrangements are one way to ensure that students interact with classmates they haven't known before. They can also further classroom belonging. When we were writing our book *Middle School: A Place to Belong and Become* (Barron & Kinney, 2018), we learned that some students found choosing their own seats stressful; it added peer pressure they'd rather not have to deal with, made them feel uncomfortable, and perpetuated established cliques. When students choose their own seats, it is likely that some will be excluded—leaving some kids feeling they don't belong. Even if no student acts out as a result of being left out, the very practice of excluding students is itself a classroom-management problem.

Students shouldn't stay in the same seat all year (or even all quarter). Mix them up on a regular basis. If your room setup allows, change the seating configuration now and then, too. Rows, groups, U-shapes, and circles all work well and give students a different perspective on the classroom (and on one another).

When students know exactly where to sit each day, especially at the beginning of the year, you eliminate the discussions, debates, and uncertainties that exist when they are left to choose or find their own seats each day. This strategy saves time, reduces chaos and disagreements, and leaves you ready to teach the class. You can make use of your seating connections (or groupings) and assign learning tasks to be done by neighbors or seating groups, which increases the possibilities for students getting to know and value one another.

Strategy 13: Inspire Class Cohesiveness

When students join together to do a project—such as create a class symbol, do a service project, or establish a tradition—they ignite and deepen the sense of themselves as a group. When everyone has an active part in the process, each student feels a little more belonging. Do at least one of these class-unity activities within the first month of school. But don't stop there. Just as with the icebreakers, use other activities to keep building and nurturing pride in "our class" all year long. When one of these projects or activities is completed, take some time for a reflective discussion on how it affected class unity.

Class Service Projects

Find a project to do together that benefits or supports others in the school community or wider community:

- Clean up the playground or cafeteria, or volunteer as a class to do a cleanup project somewhere else in the community.
- Beautify the school halls, exterior, or playground, or beautify some other space in the community.

- Collect food or toys for a community organization or clothing to donate to a homeless shelter.
- Decorate the classroom door, and pair with a younger/older class in the school to decorate theirs.
- Collect recyclable bottles and cans, and take them to a recycling center; if your state issues refunds for recyclables, donate the cash to a nonprofit organization.

Class Creations

These activities encourage students to put their heads and creative ideas together to complete a work of art.

Jigsaw art. Design a huge, blank, jigsaw puzzle with enough pieces for all students. Each person takes a piece and decorates it to contribute it to the puzzle. The puzzle can be focused on a subject area or topic (e.g., geography, math problem solving, science inquiry, PE safety), combining key concepts or steps in a process so that, when completed, the puzzle becomes a tool for learning or review. To build a sense of school community, the class could create a puzzle of the school mascot, the class crest, or the school building.

Group poetry. Write a poem together, with each person contributing a line or a pair of lines (rhyming or not). Start the lines with the same opening phrase, such as:

I wish . . .
I dreamed . . .
If it hadn't been for the invention of _____, . . .
If I could, I would change . . .
A good friend . . .
School would be a better place if . . .
More kids will feel they belong when . . .
The important thing about _____ is . . .

Using one of the phrases, each student completes several (maybe as many as 10) sentences or phrases with that starter. Students choose which ones to contribute to the class poem. The whole class could respond to the same prompt, or students might choose individual prompts.

MegaMural. Plan a hall mural that promotes the school's motto by showing actions, goals, or mindsets for students to aspire to. Find a way for all members of the class to contribute to the ideas for the mural and its execution. The goal is to allow students to draw on their strengths. Some might be talented designers but not dexterous with a paintbrush; some might gravitate to words more than visuals; some might be enlisted to coordinate who will do what, solicit others' ideas, organize supplies, or set up snacks. Find a role for everyone. Then, plan an event for the mural's unveiling.

Class Symbols

Envision, design, and compose something that reflects the spirit, values, and unity of the class—something unique to this group of students alone. Any creation that serves as a symbol for the class promotes the sense of interdependence and mutual worth for all members. For schools that are organized by teams, this is also a good team building project. Your class might develop any of the following:

- Class constitution
- Class tradition
- Class logo
- Class flag
- Class handshake
- Class crest
- Class song
- Class name

Strategy 14: Create Relationship Prescriptions

Nearly everyone has had the experience of going to a doctor and being given a prescription to help cure what ails them. In the same vein, sometimes students need to have a "prescription" in order to solve a relationship issue—and what better way to do this than to have the students write the prescription for an individual or group "illness"? When students are asked to observe and consider common relationship situations in the classroom, they can begin to envision actions that provide the foundation for respectful, positive peer relationships. Conflicts between students or small groups of students can have a significant effect on classroom management and, therefore, overall student achievement.

This strategy can be used proactively for a whole-class "prescription," but it is also very helpful as a strategy when a relationship between two or a small group of students has gone downhill. And every teacher knows the effect that can have on the atmosphere of a classroom. Here's what to do:

1. Hold a general discussion about peer relationships in the classroom. Get the dialogue started with questions such as
   — What "conditions" or relationship needs do you notice that students might be able to solve or meet (acting on their own or as a group)?
   — What behavior, attitude, or practice for relating to others would you suggest to address the situation or meet the identified need?
   — What is needed for satisfying, kind relationships in the classroom?
2. Ask the class or the students involved to identify a general issue. Or, if you're applying this activity to a specific situation, ask them to identify the specific issue or issues involved.
3. Ask students to "write a prescription"—identify a specific action that can be taken to treat the situation (see Figure 2.4's sample "prescription pad," which adds a fun touch).

FIGURE 2.4

"Rx for Peer Relationships" Template

Directions: Identify a relationship situation or need in the classroom. Then prescribe a treatment for that situation. Write the prescription as an action that can be carried out by one or more students. Include the amount, frequency, and duration of the treatment. (Tailor your directions to be age appropriate.)

Rx   Relationship Rx for (class name) _____

Date _____

Need or condition requiring treatment:

Description of treatment:

Dosage (How much?)   Frequency (How often?)

Duration (For how long?)

Expected results or side effects:

4. Have students share their prescriptions; together, make a plan for implementing them. Older students might collect and display data (e.g., graphs) to track how well the prescriptions are being followed. Younger students could gather prescriptions together to make a "menu" for healthy class living. (If you are using this process for just a pair of or a few students involved in a particular incident, they would share and discuss the prescriptions just among themselves.)

5. Plan follow-up visits to see how the "medicine" is working. Analyze the data collected. What are the effects of the different "medications"? Which prescriptions worked, and which situations need a different prescription? Guide a class discussion that draws conclusions about any changes to the "relationship health" in the class.

Strategy 15: Take Humor Seriously

When Patti was a principal, a teacher in her school had an awesome sense of humor and kept staff members in stitches much of the time. But she hadn't ever observed him using humor in the classroom. When she asked about it, he said he was afraid to use it because his students might get out of control. She encouraged him to lighten up a bit and share this wonderful gift with his students. The atmosphere in this teacher's classroom warmed up considerably as he relaxed around the students, and the loss of control he feared never happened.

Humor in the classroom is more than just making students laugh. It can increase the feeling of belongingness, improve class cohesiveness, generate positive energy, defuse a potential problem from escalating, strengthen relationships, make lessons more engaging, and help everyone cope with stress. However, put-down or "insult" humor weakens group togetherness and hinders feelings of belonging. Teachers who attempt to use humor to control and target individual students—by making fun of their ignorance, appearance, or beliefs—will have a drastic and negative effect on classroom management.

Proper use of humor is serious business, so use the following guidelines to ensure that your classroom humor stays on the right track.

Connect Humor to Content

Humor that relates to content you're teaching is almost always appropriate—funny stories, cartoons, and riddles and puns ("What do we call a dead parrot? A *polygon!*") that connect with the content make students laugh or smile. Because humor can increase levels of attention and interest, it's a good way to keep students engaged and involved with the lesson. Here are a few ways to incorporate humor into your classroom routines:

- Have a "Joke of the Day."
- Read a funny short story or poem.
- Pose riddles.
- Put a puzzle on the board for students to solve.
- Share a funny quote.
- Insert a humorous question or two into a test (but don't count it toward the grade).
- Encourage students to write content-based jokes (screen them first before sharing with the class!).
- Wear a funny costume or come to school dressed as someone famous in your content area.

Don't Try Too Hard

It's painful to watch someone who is trying to be funny but isn't. If humor is not one of your strengths, tap into the humor of others via a "quote of the day," cartoons, comics, or video clips. Our friend Jack Berckemeyer, a natural humorist, former teacher, and popular speaker, often shares ways to use humor to build relationships with students and throw some engaging twists into classroom management. In *Managing the Madness* (2017), he gives examples of chewing out an imaginary student in the class to get the attention of his "real" students or turning to the whiteboard and loudly asking its advice on what to do. Although this isn't what either of us would naturally do, it works for him and for many other teachers. Be willing to stretch and grow in the use of humor, but don't move too far out of your comfort zone and try ideas that just don't fit your style.

Keep It Positive

Any attempt at humor that manipulates, denigrates, ridicules, mocks others, or is offensive humor that is lewd or perpetuates racism, sexism, or other isms should *never* be used in the classroom. It's the rare educator who can effectively (and appropriately) use humor that is sarcastic. Even when directed at a student who understands and enjoys the use of sarcasm, it can backfire, because others in the room may take it seriously. The truth is there's never a real need to use sarcasm in the classroom.

Think It Through

Laurie's experience team-teaching a combined 10th grade world literature and world history course taught her a lot about the power of humor—and the need to anticipate its consequences. When teaching about the Battle of Thermopylae, her teaching partner, Steve, insisted they act out the parts of the key players. Steve played the role of the eventually victorious Xerxes. They particularly enjoyed reenacting the famous "Our arrows will block out the sun" part of the story, which included Laurie losing the battle. The next day, she and a few students were plotting Troy's revenge. Suddenly, a student named Paul grabbed a huge bag of mini-pretzels, ran up to Steve, raised the open bag toward the classroom's overhead lights, and tossed the pretzels into the air—a rain of salty "arrows." What began as fun and games ended with 500 miniature pretzels all over the classroom. The teachers spent the next half hour cleaning up, with Laurie apologizing profusely and explaining how her humor got out of hand.

All this to say, use of humor can misfire and create unexpected issues. Always try to think ahead.

Strategy 16: Keep Up the Kid-Watching

As you and your students get in the belonging mindset, your "sensors" will sharpen. But sometimes teachers are so focused on covering content, helping students stay on task, adapting instruction for individual students, and dealing with unexpected incidents that those sensors get blocked or dulled.

Become intentional about the practice of "kid-watching"—that is, watch kids when they don't know you're watching. You can learn a great deal about your students when you become more mindful about how they work and interact with others. Kid-watching is also a great way to identify and head off potential trouble before it becomes a management issue.

Stealthy Observation

Tune in to what students say to and about one another. Listen to the rumblings among students in classroom corners, hallways, playgrounds, the lunchroom, and restrooms. Be alert to conversations that stop when you get near or when another student comes near. Look closely at individual students for behavioral and emotional signs of exclusion, discomfort, or anxiety. Take note of body language, and watch to detect whether a student is struggling, upset, angry, or withdrawing.

When your stealthy observation alerts you to something, first address it privately with the individual student. Try to get clarity about what is going on. Keep some notes about any difficulties you discover, and make plans for necessary actions. The fact that you've noticed is what will make it possible for you to help.

Quiet Affirmations

Develop a habit of catching students doing things right. Watch for those moments when a student is helping someone else, encouraging a fellow student, being kind, or just showing any of the dozens of actions or attitudes you've all discussed as being responsible, respectful, and cooperative.

Make a point of privately affirming these actions. Be specific, describing what you've seen them doing and noting one or more positive outcomes (e.g., "Explaining that process to Cyndy helped her get confident about how to solve other problems with division of fractions. Thank you."). Your affirmation should highlight what the student did that was responsible to himself or helpful to another; be careful not to convey the message that the student was somehow doing you a favor. *Positive behaviors are responsible actions students undertake for their own or others' well-being;* they are not about pleasing you. Of course, if a student does something kind directly *for* you, say, "Thanks. I really appreciate your words [or help]."

Affirmations in Print

Some schools and teachers share their kid-watching observations with students' families; they send an electronic communication or postcard home relating a compliment or summary of what they witnessed. One school that we know keeps a stack of stamped postcards in the office so that any staff member who personally sees a commendable action can easily send a positive note. In most cases, this has a profound effect on school belonging for both students and their families.

Laurie's current district distributes postcards at the monthly staff meeting. Every teacher chooses two students and then writes each one a postcard that's related to the topic or theme of the month. The office staff adds the address and stamp and mails the postcard to the student. Here are few examples of topics to consider.

- **September: "Welcome!"** Choose two students who are new to your community or school or who have had a major life change over the summer. Welcome these students to your class, and tell them how happy you are to have them in your class.
- **November: "Kindness Spotting."** Choose two students who are good citizens, classmates, and friends to others. Let these students know how important their acts of kindness and inclusiveness are to others and that you notice the efforts they make on a daily basis. This is a great time to show thankfulness!
- **February: "Most Improved."** Choose two students in your class who have shown significant gains in attitude, achievement, attention, attendance, and so on. Let these students know how proud you are of the improvement they've made.

You'll notice that all of the recognition and affirmation we recommend is private—not public. Public praise, regardless of how well intentioned, can be uncomfortable for the praised and for surrounding students who are not praised. It can easily backfire and undermine the belonging you seek to create.

Strategy 17: Strengthen Bonds with Students' Families

As the year progresses, don't forget about those family contacts you initiated early in the school year (see Strategy 5, p. 19). The relationships you build with students and their families increase all-around belonging for your students and continue to affect classroom management. These relationships also benefit both families and teachers. Contacting families with needs, praises, or problems is easier when you have already established a caring relationship. In your early communications, you let them know that you are accessible and that they can count on you to be there. If difficulties arise, they'll be able to trust that you will be a fair, caring advocate for their child. Here are some recommendations for maintaining a trusting connection with families throughout the school year:

- **Within the first two weeks of school,** send at least one group email or letter. Tell families something about what's been happening in the classroom— what kids are learning and accomplishing. Give them ideas of things they can do to reinforce their student's learning. These group communications should build on the communications you've already sent individual students' families.

- **Within the first three or four weeks,** send at least one individual electronic communication or notecard to each student's family. Tell them something positive or encouraging about their child. This can be something the student created, accomplished, learned, or is learning. Or it can just mention a quality the student has that you value or that contributes to the class. Share something you think the student would be proud to have the parent hear.

- **Throughout the year,** keep up with communication! If you have a self-contained classroom, this is something that is easier to do even more often. Some elementary teachers send individual messages as often as once or twice a week. If you have a large number of students, try to let parents hear from you once or twice a month.

- **When a parent happens to stop by the school,** take advantage of this opportunity. Just saying "hi" to a parent you see in the hallway, making a casual comment about their child, or inviting the parent into your classroom can strengthen bonds with families. If you keep portfolio crates or folders of student work in your room, students can "show off" their work when their families are in the school. Simple communication sends the message "I care about your child."

Student-Led Conferences

Traditionally, parents have attended conferences with teachers while students were left home to wonder what was being discussed. Early in our careers as teachers, we communicated with parents or guardians during conferences, but it always felt like something was missing—*the student!* If your school has not initiated student-led conferences, we encourage you to consider adding this practice to your repertoire.

The communication that occurs during a student-led conference is powerful and sends the message that you are working in partnership with the families for the benefit of their children. Having students share their successes or acknowledge their challenges encourages them to own the behavior (positive or negative) and take responsibility for continuing or decreasing that behavior. There is more focus on what the student has (or has not) done and therefore less "blame" (again, good or not so good) on the teacher. With the common goal of helping students be successful, these conferences help strengthen your bond with students and their families. For more on this topic, see Patti's book *Fostering Student Accountability Through Student-Led Conferences* (Kinney, 2012).

Extracurricular Communications

Sometimes it's difficult to involve and communicate with parents or guardians whose own school experiences were not altogether positive, who have a work schedule that makes it difficult to engage, or who are from a culture or speak a language that makes communication difficult. We've found that even when a parent or guardian does not get involved with formal channels of communication, they often find a way to be involved in their student's extracurricular activities (e.g., sports, the performing arts).

Therefore, make it a point to try to attend students' extracurricular events with a goal of communicating with families. Some of the best conversations we've had with parents over the years have taken place during a football or basketball game or after a chorus or band concert. When you make the extra effort to get to know students outside the classroom and communicate with their parents or guardians about nonclassroom activities, you demonstrate that your caring extends beyond the classroom walls. This is solid reinforcement for the student–teacher relationships you've begun to establish.

3

Belonging Thrives on Safety

How can I belong when I feel scared most of the time that I'm at school?
a 7th grader

This chapter invites you to explore the many forms of safety students can experience in school and offers practices for heightening students' sense of safety. It also examines many "tried and true" classroom management practices through the lens of promoting belonging. Strategies discussed include reflecting on school policies and practices that affect safety, enlisting students as partners in identifying and responding to safety concerns, employing practices that promote mental and emotional safety, and working with challenging behaviors and issues that can threaten the safety of all.

Many students arrive at school each day worried about their emotional or physical safety. Up to a third of school-age children in the United States report some form of bullying or perceived threat at school (Card & Hodges, 2008; Robers, Zhang, Truman, & Snyder, 2012; Walton, 2005). They might be beset by worries and fears related to past or ongoing trauma, something going on at home, their personal identity, or the tumultuous and uncertain state of the world—any of which can leave them feeling extra-vulnerable in a school climate that feels less than secure.

Students who perceive their school settings as chaotic or unsafe are not able to function fully. They can experience emotional distress, loneliness, depression, low self-esteem, and decline in academic performance (Goodenow & Grady, 1993; Hawker & Boulton, 2000; Ladd & Wardrop, 2001). When students feel disconnected, their belongingness is threatened; the less they feel that they belong, in turn, the less safe they feel (Derosier & Newcity, 2005).

In order to thrive academically, socially, and emotionally, students need to feel safe and secure. Impressions of safety come from many sources—a clean and orderly school; a low incidence of physical, social, or emotional violence; clear, consistent guidelines for behavior and predictable routines; healthy ways to dialogue about differences in viewpoint; and caring adults who are available and can be trusted to protect students. To achieve all this, teachers and other adults in the school must be aware of the many challenges students are facing, take efforts to protect them from all forms of discrimination, and promote school policies and procedures that prioritize safety and social justice.

Strategy 18: Fine-Tune School Safety Measures

Plain and simple: A lack of emotional and physical safety at school is a detriment to any student's belongingness and increases the likelihood of behavior issues.

Schools have plans for the physical safety of staff and students: procedures and drills for events such as fire, earthquakes, and other natural disasters as well as school intrusions. As a result of the COVID-19 pandemic, these plans have evolved to include safety measures that prevent the spread of dangerous diseases. Teachers and school administrators also think about and plan for physical safety in the cafeteria, hallways, classrooms, laboratories, shop or kitchen areas, gymnasiums and locker rooms, bathrooms, and other spaces, endeavoring to ensure these places are clean, uncluttered, and free of safety hazards. As caring adults in the school, we can't take away all external threats, but we *can* show our commitment to physical safety by conscientiously following school safety procedures.

In addition to these more obvious efforts, we must also be sure to take students' fears and traumatic experiences seriously and create ways for students to express them, discuss them, and gain a measure of assurance. And we must consistently communicate to all students that the adults in this school care about their safety and work hard to keep everyone safe.

Although students (and teachers) do worry about the potential for the kind of in-school violence that we see in the news, on an average school day, many students worry more about being bullied or threatened because of their appearance, their home language, their race, a disability, or any number of other reasons. They worry about being the target of gossip, being teased, or being humiliated or excluded. For thousands of students (or more), school is a scary place. Plenty of these threats take place in classrooms, even in sight or hearing of the supervising adult. More often, however, they happen out of sight or hearing of the adults—on the playground or other outside areas and in halls, cafeterias, locker rooms, and bathrooms. Some kids are terrified before they even get to school, worried about what might happen on their walking route or on the bus (Barrington, 2020).

Safety is intertwined with everything that happens for you and your students. It's connected to your relationships with students, relationships between students, classroom management, the classroom culture, academic activities, and all your efforts to help students belong. Unfortunately, some behaviors of the adults in schools—their attitudes, gestures, facial expressions, procedures, actions, inactions, and words—can impede students' safety. The upside is that the deliberate actions you take to promote all kinds of safety make a substantial difference in your students' school experience.

Your classroom management and plans for class climate undoubtedly include procedures, attitudes, and behaviors to address threats to safety that exist inside the school. Here are some ways to keep physical and emotional safety in the forefront, with the goal of enhancing students' sense of safety and belonging.

Conduct a School Safety Checkup

Assurance of safety for students starts on the first day of school and has to be carefully maintained throughout the year. On your own or with colleagues, do your own safety checkup, perhaps modeled after the one in Figure 3.1, which is based on key principles of school safety. Are the safety measures in your school or classroom sufficiently comprehensive? What aspects of safety might need more attention? Scan through your checklist once a week or so to keep safety on your radar. Add items to your list as new issues arise.

Consider sharing your checklist with students. Individually, or in groups, students can highlight actions they believe should be top priorities. Encourage them to add any statements or behaviors they think are missing. Be brave enough to let students comment on elements of the list that they do not witness consistently.

FIGURE 3.1

School Safety Checkup

1. Safety starts with the "feel" of the place.

Components	✔ Yes	✔ No
Are all areas of the school and classroom neat, clean, pleasant, and orderly?		
Do classroom arrangements give as much space as possible to move and learn?		
Do seating assignments minimize clashes or other discomfort?		
Are school policies on bullying and other unsafe, discriminatory, or mean behaviors stated and consistently adhered to by adults?		
Are school health policies and practices stated and consistently enforced and adhered to by adults?		
Do students know there is adequate supervision, particularly in the places where mistreatment is likely to take place?		
Do supervising adults have and use their authority (consistently and effectively) to act in keeping students safe from other students?		
Are students' fears about safety taken seriously?		
Do students have safe opportunities to share their concerns?		
Are families warmly welcomed to the school and given chances to be involved?		

Notes/Actions Needed:

2. Effective, positive classroom management is a key factor in students' safety.

Components	✔ Yes	✔ No
Is mutual respect a top priority?		
Are routines, schedules, guidelines, limits, expectations, and consequences clearly established, predictable, and consistently followed?		
Are expectations and consequences equitable?		
Are students expected to speak positively to one another and taught how to do this?		
Are students given advance notice of changes in schedules, expectations, and assignments?		
Is misbehavior handled privately between teacher and student?		

Notes/Actions Needed:

3. Acquiring and practicing social-emotional skills helps students cope with feelings of insecurity.

Components	✔ Yes	✔ No
Do students have a secure and private way to ask questions, ask for help, or report problems?		
Are students given lessons in self-advocacy and other skills of self-regulation and self-control?		
Do students receive instruction in social–emotional skills?		
Are students taught ways to respond to teasing and bullying, as either a victim or a bystander?		
Do students learn strategies for helping to keep situations from escalating into violence?		
Do students have frequent experiences that help them feel in control?		

Notes/Actions Needed:

(continued)

FIGURE 3.1
School Safety Checkup (*continued*)

4. Comfortable relationships with trusted adults help students feel safe.		
Components	**✔ Yes**	**✔ No**
Are adults in the school approachable, caring, and kind?		
Do staff members say "please" and "thank you"?		
Are teachers confident, showing joy and excitement about their jobs?		
Are teachers truthful and trustworthy—keeping their word, following through, and doing what they promise?		
Are teachers calm during crises, transitions, or chaos?		
Do teachers give positive responses and encouragement?		
Are teachers "on top of" what is going on in the classroom or other school locations?		
Can teachers be counted on to consistently protect students from verbal teasing, name calling, and being bothered, bullied, demeaned, or intentionally excluded?		
Do teachers actively protect students from discrimination based on gender, race, ethnicity, religion, physical appearance or capabilities, academic achievement, sexual orientation, political views, socioeconomic status, or family involvement in school?		
Do teachers have a deep knowledge of the unique learning needs of each student and demonstrably help them succeed academically?		
Do teachers periodically check their assumptions about students and actively work to uncover their blind spots?		
Do teachers reflect regularly on their practice to recognize implicit bias and address and prevent new biases?		
Do teachers respect the confidentiality of student comments?		
Do teachers protect the safety of students' questions and contributions in learning situations?		
Do teachers use humor appropriately and sarcasm cautiously?		
Do teachers keep open, respectful communication with students' families?		
Notes/Actions Needed:		

Tune Up Your Safety Radar

Start with your own self-awareness. Consult resources like Vernita Mayfield's *Cultural Competence Now* (2020) to guide an examination of your own beliefs and biases surrounding race and ethnicity, and dig into the biases you may have related to gender and sexual orientation, religious identity, physical differences, academic achievement, and students' socioeconomic status (see also Pate, 2020; Sadker, Sadker, & Zittleman, 2009). Think about how to measure family support or involvement in school and how the presence or absence of family involvement affects your attitudes and behaviors (see Breiseth, 2016). After a close scrutiny of your beliefs and biases, turn the microscope to examination of your actions. You are a model; students notice what you do and what you say. Do you demonstrate the "safe" behaviors on the checkup list in Figure 3.1? Do you model kindness, acceptance, and belief in students? Figure 3.2 , with its list of behaviors to avoid at all costs, provides additional guidance.

FIGURE 3.2

Behaviors to Avoid

Many uncomfortable, potentially unsafe experiences for students can be prevented by scrupulous avoidance of inappropriate teacher attitudes and behaviors.

✔ DON'T assume things about who students are and why they do what they do.

✔ DON'T judge a student by the behavior or history of a sibling or other family member.

✔ DON'T project any messages that a student is incapable of something or is being lazy.

✔ DON'T stereotype, ridicule, bully, exclude, deride, or abandon any student—ever.

✔ DON'T put down or show dislike, resentment, or disgust toward any student—ever (even subtly).

✔ DON'T dismiss or diminish a student's question.

✔ DON'T discuss another student, parent, or teacher within hearing of a student.

✔ DON'T yell, threaten, curse, or silently fume.

✔ DON'T compare students with one another.

✔ DON'T gossip about students or anyone else in the school.

✔ DON'T post opinions on social media that have anything to do with school, students, colleagues, or parents (unless they are carefully and clearly positive).

Students are counting on you for their safety, so you must be vigilant. Keep your eyes and ears open. Watch for students sitting alone. Notice what's going on with groups and individuals. Pay attention to nonverbal signs about students' levels of safety. Be aware of a dramatic change in a student's demeanor or behaviors. Don't overlook signs of dangers or discomfort. Use your sensors to identify when you need to help students feel connected and to prevent classroom management issues before they arise.

Strategy 19: Enlist Students as Partners in Safety

John Nori, an educator friend of ours, shared the following experience, which, as he said, "serves as a powerful reminder to all educators to listen to your students!"

> When the "Beltway sniper" was active in the Washington, DC, area in 2002, I stopped at the middle school where I had previously been the principal to visit with the current principal.

The kids were shaken by the shootings; the sniper had even been in our town. The principal gathered an informal group of 8th graders and asked them what the teachers and administrators were doing right and wrong in their efforts to keep everyone safe. Students volunteered many things that individual teachers were saying and doing that helped them feel safe. When they were clearly running out of things to say, and the principal started to write hall passes to get them back to class, one student blurted out, "What about the windows?"— pointing to the windows above the door and on both sides of the doors.

The principal said, "Duh! Why didn't I think of that?" and asked how they should be covered. The girl who had spoken up originally suggested artwork, so that's what they did. (Personal communication, July 7, 2020)

Because many threats to students' emotional and physical safety come from other students (see U.S. Department of Health and Human Services, 2020), responsibility for safety at school can't be left in the hands of adults alone. Students must learn how to look out for their own safety and for the safety of others. Include them in safety discussions and in safety plans, actions, and age-appropriate training. Strategy 18 suggests that you consider sharing the school safety checkup list with your students and inviting students to join the conversation about safety factors inside the school community. Continue engaging students in the process by focusing on *their* role. Help them understand how they contribute to both safe and unsafe conditions, the difference safety makes, and how to be proactive about safety—and not just physical safety but emotional and social safety as well.

In addition to following established school protocols, students can also identify specific actions they can take to increase safety. Assign them the task of planning the real steps they will take. The steps may be spread over a series of days or classes. Although the process may work best for groups such as a homeroom, an advisory class, a team of students, or a school's student leadership council or student government association, you should be able to adapt it for your grade level, content area, or setting.

Step 1: Present the Challenge to Students

Assign students to pairs. Assign half of the pair groups to make a list titled "Ways Students Contribute to a Lack of Safety for Themselves or Others at School," and the other half to make a list titled "Ways Students Can Keep Themselves and

Others Safe at School." Remind students that "safety" includes emotional and social safety as well as physical safety. Ask student pairs to brainstorm ideas and come to a consensus about what they see to be the 10 most critical items.

Next, join pairs assigned the same list into groups of six. Ask this new group to discuss and combine their lists to arrive at a consensus of 8 to 10 items to keep.

Step 2: Reach Class Consensus on Priorities

With all students together, share lists from the groups of six. Working first with students' lists of actions that cause a lack of safety, review and discuss the results of their small-group work, conclusions they reached, and the implications or consequences of the actions they've identified.

Use a process of prioritizing items to come to a group consensus about which ones most need their attention. They might identify actions that are most frequent or most harmful. Or they might choose actions with which they're most likely to be successful. Create an all-class list of their top 10 items.

Repeat the process to develop an all-class consensus on ways students can keep themselves and others safe at school.

Step 3: Identify Next Steps

Ask students, "What will we do with the ideas we've gathered? What can we do—as individuals and together—in our classroom?" Ask them each to write down two actions that they will personally commit to do consistently to improve safety for themselves and others; then place students in groups to combine their ideas. Then, regroup as a whole class to refine a list of agreed-upon commitments for safety. This will be a set of 5 to 10 actions they believe they can carry out consistently, either in a classroom or in the school as a whole.

Step 4: Commit to the Commitments

Let students devise a way to put their commitments into writing in a contract or promise (see the sample template in Figure 3.3). The agreement can be seen as a group safety commitment, but each student should sign on for personal responsibility. Statements should be worded in terms of what they *will do* or *will refrain from doing* and include responsibilities both for personal safety and for contributing to the safety of others. Discuss ways students can help one another, and

---

FIGURE 3.3

Template for a Student Safety Commitment

I, _____ [individual name], a member of _____ [group or class name], commit to consistently taking these actions to protect my own safety at school:

I will _____

I will _____

I will _____

I, _____ [individual name], a member of _____ [group or class name], commit to consistently taking these actions to lessen threats or help protect the safety of others at school:

I will _____

I will _____

I will _____

I will review this contract and evaluate my progress on the following dates: _____

Date: _____   Signature: _____

---

ways you can help them, keep these commitments. Set a process and date or time period for reflecting on or evaluating their success with these commitments.

Be sure to find time throughout the school year for students to discuss their experiences trying to keep these commitments and the implications or consequences of making and keeping the commitments. Be open to working with students to expand or change their commitments as they deem necessary.

Strategy 20: Define and Demonstrate Values

From their earliest years of schooling, students hear teachers and school officials talk about respect, responsibility, cooperation, and other attitudes and behaviors that help promote a feeling of safety. "Be responsible." "Cooperate." "Be respectful." All too often, however, teachers assume that students know what these words mean and understand how to translate them into behavior.

Educators should not assume, even in the upper grade levels, that students really know what we mean and expect when we tell them to be respectful, cooperative, supportive, or tolerant. Students need to define, recognize, and practice specific behaviors that show these concepts in action. They need to know what to do—or not do. In addition, they need to understand the reasons for these actions.

Identify Prosocial Behaviors

Our friend Ross Burkhardt and his teaching partner developed a list of 13 *distinctions*, words that label the beliefs and values that should guide student behavior: "acknowledgment, appreciation, commitment, communication, compassion, contribution, cooperation, individuality, respect, responsibility, risk, support, and trust" (2003, pp. 31, 40–41). They developed lessons around these distinctions— lessons to help students define the meanings of the concepts, recognize how they look in practice, and consider the effect they have on their lives.

Another friend, Theresa Atchison, adapted Ross's idea. With the help of their students, Theresa and her teammates created a list they called "Distinctions of Integrity." Early in the year, they discussed and defined each concept. Throughout the year, they infused these values into class discussions, assignments, and a behavior reflection sheet to help students be more thoughtful about their choices and behaviors. The goals were to build community, increase a sense of belonging for everyone, and help students see that the norms established for their school lives had relevance in the classroom and beyond.

Give Lessons on Distinctions

There are many ways for students to learn about, promote, and practice the distinct qualities critical to a healthy school community. Engage your students in defining and demonstrating such qualities and the differences and nuances that set them apart from one another.

In our adaptation of our friends' work, we've developed a lesson for engaging with one distinction at a time, which can be adapted to fit the grade level(s) or group you teach. With younger students, work with the whole class to draw out definitions, details, and evidence of the quality. Older students can work in pairs or small groups to "dissect" the concept. Repeat this type of lesson with other distinctions throughout the early months of the school year. Reinforce the behaviors and understandings all year long.

Step 1: Choose a quality. Start with one quality that you know must be included on your list. Project or write the word. Ask students to say it out loud and to think about what it means. Give them a minute to jot down a thought or action or draw a picture that gives an idea about its meaning. This requires each student to put some individual attention to the concept before joining in a group discussion or activity.

Step 2: Explain the goal of the lesson. Tell students that you know they've been told, for example, to be cooperative. Tell them that, today, they'll be putting "cooperation" under a microscope to examine its full meaning, including how they know it when they see it, experience it, or work with someone else.

Step 3: Collect ideas. Give each pair or small group of students a template to collect and record their ideas about the meaning of the quality you're focusing on (see Figure 3.4 for a model). With younger students, work through the questions together, and make a record of the outcomes for everyone to see.

FIGURE 3.4
___

"Anatomy of a Quality" Template

Focus on_____

Class:_____ Date: _____

Student Names: _____

What does this term mean? (Write your definition.)

What *words* can someone use to demonstrate this quality?

What *actions* can someone take to demonstrate this quality?

What *body language* (facial expressions or gestures) demonstrates this quality?

How does it feel when you experience this quality through someone's words, actions, or body language?

Step 4: Share ideas and understandings. Reconvene the class and ask groups to share their ideas. Agree on a group definition of the term. Have a recorder write a list of ways it shows up in action and communication. For example, students might say, "Cooperation means working together" or "Cooperation is being kind to one another." Create and display a poster with this list.

Step 5: Demonstrate the quality. On a regular basis (daily or weekly), ask students to identify one item on the list that they will deliberately demonstrate. Eventually, many of the actions will become habits. This choice can be a group consensus or individual choice.

Step 6: Deepen the quality. Continue to talk about the quality, affirm it when it happens, add more evidence of it to the list, and reflect on how it feels when it happens.

Step 7: Expand the lessons. At some point, repeat this process with its opposite term (e.g., *uncooperative*). When the list is written, the group can contract or agree with one another that the items on that list will be banned from the classroom.

Strategy 21: Ensure That Everyone Is Seen and Heard

When students do not feel they are seen, heard, or valued, they can become isolated, alone, and frustrated—and as a result they can turn to self-harm or harming others, emotionally or physically. Ensuring every student feels they belong will decrease feelings of seclusion and loneliness. And belonging soars when students step into a classroom or school where it's clear others truly want to know and hear them.

Respect is an integral part of building a sense of belonging in the classroom; it maximizes a safe and consistent climate that is rich for learning and minimizes disruptive behaviors. Planning specific practices and activities to ensure that everyone is known for who they are (not some assumption or stereotype) and are heard, with many chances to speak their ideas and opinions, builds respect. Students who feel unnoticed, unimportant, or unheard in a classroom can become defiant and disruptive. Or they may withdraw into themselves, losing connection to others.

Exemplars for "Respect"

For a bit of a variation (or addition) to the "anatomy of a quality" exercise in Strategy 20, spotlight "respect" with this strategy. Begin by defining for students the word *exemplar:* a typical example or ideal model of something. Brainstorm characteristics of exemplars for different categories (e.g., "How would you describe an exemplar of a good leader? a friend? a book report?"). Then divide students into groups of three or four, and have each group create a three-column chart with the headings "What respect looks like," "What respect sounds like," and "What respect feels like." Ask the groups to write down five characteristics or exemplars for each column. Have each group share their chart and add their examples to a larger classroom chart. Look for commonalities, and use them to create a poster for the classroom that combines students' thoughts.

"Don't Laugh at Me"

Ask students questions similar to these:

- Have you ever watched *America's Funniest Home Videos?*
- What type of situations do you think are the funniest?
- Why do you think people laugh when someone has an accident, doesn't do something the "right" way, or makes a big mistake?
- Have you ever been in a situation where others laughed at you? How did you feel?
- Have you ever laughed at or made fun of someone? Why or why not?
- When is it OK to laugh at someone? When is it not OK?

Peter, Paul, and Mary, an American folk group founded in the 1961, are famous for many songs, including "Puff, the Magic Dragon." In 1998, the trio recorded the song "Don't Laugh at Me," which the organization Operation Respect has used to help schools combat bullying and resolve conflicts. We suggest that you search for "Operation Respect, Don't Laugh at Me Video" on the internet (Operation Respect, n.d.). You'll be led to their website and a video of the song's lyrics. The lyrics serve as the narrative, while you see people of all ages and abilities in a variety of situations. Show "Don't Laugh at Me" to your class, and discuss how students feel about it, what it leads them to think about, and how it might impact ways they treat others. The website with the video offers other suggestions for using it to teach about respect.

Group Agreements

Have students work together—in pairs, small groups, or as one big group—to create a set of agreements about how members of the classroom (including the teacher) can treat one another with respect and guarantee that everyone's voice is valued. Begin by asking them to complete these thoughts:

- If we want to be sure that every person in our classroom feels seen as valuable and knows that others are interested in him or her, then we will . . . .

- If we want to be sure that every voice in our classroom is important and respected, then we will . . . .

In Laurie's district, 6th grade students and teachers write and sign a pledge promising to do their best, be kind, listen to one another, and so on. The signed pledge is then displayed in the hallway for all to see. It would be easy to adapt the commitments made in Figure 3.3 to create a classroom pledge to post in your classroom.

Students as Advisors on School "Business"

The more you can incorporate as much and as many student voices into non-academic school matters, the more students will feel respected and believe that their opinions are heard and valued.

For example, when Patti's school was planning to build a playground structure for the middle school students to use during lunch or break time, there was pushback by some adults who didn't believe a playground was necessary for this age group. Patti pulled together a group of 8th graders, gave them the catalog for the company they were using, and asked them to come up with ideas for equipment that students would find fun to use. The students came back with their recommendations, the structure was built based on their ideas, and it's been crowded with students ever since.

In another school district we've visited, the school board holds a daytime meeting at both the middle and high schools. Classes of students attend, the board explains their "job" for the district, and students are encouraged to ask members questions or express concerns. Questions have ranged from "Why can't we wear pajamas to school?" to "Our class sizes are getting bigger every year, and our teachers can't get around to help everyone. What are you going to do about that?"

So what can you do?

- Check out the National Student Council's program Raising Student Voice and Participation (RSVP) at www.natstuco.org, which provides a structured process to identify and address school issues through student viewpoints.
- Establish a leadership program that incorporates as many students as possible. Student council is a popular choice, but it should be structured so the voices of many students are heard, not just a few or the same ones. Some

schools offer a rotating elective, so different students are involved in school leadership each quarter or term.

- Start a "Lunch with the Principal" program to give small groups of students a chance to talk one-on-one with school administrators.
- Create a "natural helpers" group to deal with conflicts or student bullying. Identify students from all cross-sections of the school (including those who have been involved with bullying), provide them with conflict resolution training, and then ask them to help students resolve issues.

At Laurie's middle school, the student leadership council met monthly to provide input on grade- and school-level needs and decisions. Sometimes the topics were serious (bullying, class schedules), and sometimes they were seemingly trivial (lunch menus, transitions between classes). Teachers were asked to choose 10 students from their grade level: 5 who were natural, positive leaders and 5 who were sometimes or often negative leaders. The group was diverse in terms of academic profiles, race, and gender—designed to include comprehensive representation natural at this very diverse school. Choosing student leaders who had displayed negative leadership may seem risky, but when those students were given positive tasks to complete and opportunities for input, teachers saw significant changes. Positive behaviors gradually replaced the negative ones.

Strategy 22: Handle the Big Stuff

Students and their families need to see that it is important to you that difficult situations and unstable relationships are dealt with in a timely and effective manner. High (but realistic) expectations, consistently maintained, are basic to a student's feeling of safety and nourish belonging. Students must be able to trust that their teachers and other adults in the school will be on top of troublesome behavior and not let things get out of hand.

The vast majority of the strategies in this book will work with most students. However, some students have serious emotional or behavioral challenges and need more intensive strategies. Some students don't (or won't) follow the procedures. Some students can erupt at any time. Some students chronically cause disturbances.

Here are some things to consider when nothing else seems to work. These suggestions are intended to give you additional ideas to consider when you are faced with handling the "big stuff."

Understanding Adverse Childhood Experiences

Mental health issues are one of the top concerns in education today. They profoundly influence students' experiences and behaviors in classrooms. Over the decades we've worked in education, we've observed that a significant number of students have been in unfortunate situations of experiencing trauma in their lives, and it feels as if these numbers have only increased across all age groups.

The U.S. Centers for Disease Control (CDC) and Kaiser Permanente's landmark study (Felitti et al., 1998) on adverse childhood experiences (ACEs) concluded negative experiences during childhood negatively affect one's health and well-being throughout life. Many schools and mental health care providers continue to use the ACE Study to learn more about their students and youth patients. The ACE Study measured the most common types of childhood trauma (e.g., abuse, neglect, household dysfunction, substance abuse, divorce) and assigned points for the occurrence of each. Adults with higher ACE scores as children are more likely to abuse alcohol and drugs, more likely to forgo physical activity, and more likely to exhibit high levels of absenteeism at work. They are also more likely to experience physical and mental health issues and more likely to attempt suicide (Felitti et al., 1998; Starecheski, 2015).

Identifying current trauma can help schools and teachers understand the landscape of children's lives and how trauma may affect their school functioning. It also offers an opportunity for educators to work to deter those negative adult outcomes.

Implementing Trauma-Informed Practices

Although a higher ACE score can be very concerning, many students with high ACE scores go on to be happy, healthy adults. There are proven interventions. *Fostering Resilient Learners* (2016) and *Relationship, Responsibility, and Regulation* (2018), both by Kristin Souers and Pete Hall, offer a variety of approaches to working with students affected by trauma, including a focus on building resilience in students. Understanding some practices to use in your classroom enhances your ability to help all students feel they belong, including those who have had traumatic experiences, and help you maintain a well-managed classroom.

Using Restorative Practices

The International Institute for Restorative Practices (IIRP) defines *restorative practices* as "an emerging social science that studies how to strengthen relationships between individuals as well as social connections within communities" (2020, para. 2). At one IIRP conference, its president explained,

> The fundamental unifying hypothesis of restorative practices is disarmingly simple: that human beings are happier, more cooperative and productive, and more likely to make positive changes in their behavior when those in positions of authority do things *with* them, rather than *to* them or *for* them. This hypothesis maintains that the punitive and authoritarian *to* mode and the permissive and paternalistic *for* mode are not as effective as the restorative, participatory, engaging *with* mode. If this restorative hypothesis is valid, then it has significant implications for many disciplines. (Wachtel & McCold, 2004, para. 2; emphases in original)

Certainly, education is one of those areas for which restorative practices have "significant implications." Restorative justice—what we're aiming for when we institute restorative practices in a school—offers a respectful and fair alternative to punitive discipline.

Remember these key principles:

- Restorative practices are proactive and not reactive.
- Restorative practices create an environment where students can express their feelings—instead of avoiding them, withdrawing from others, or attacking themselves or others.
- Restorative practices give students safe and respectful places and ways to express and move beyond shame, blame, embarrassment, and grief.
- Restorative practices use circles or other groups where students and adults talk through issues, incidents, and differences.

Restorative practices also use processes that all students can recognize as fair; in schools, this means including the following elements:

- **Engagement.** Students are invited to take part in discussions; their ideas and opinions are taken seriously, and they are involved in decisions that affect them.

- **Explanation.** Teachers and administrators explain a policy or decision before it is implemented and provide the reasoning behind it to everyone who is in any way affected by the decision.
- **Clarity.** The explanation given is crystal clear. Everyone involved understands what will happen and the expectations for each person (Kim & Mauborgne, 2003; Wachtel & McCold, 2004).

Students are more likely to cooperate with a system or with authorities when the process seems fair. And students are more likely to believe a process is fair when they are involved in it and see that their experiences, feelings, and opinions make a difference. A main principle of restorative practices is to approach an issue *with* the student or students. When students misbehave, make a bad decision, or display behavior that negatively affects themselves or others, take time to talk *with* them, not *at* them. Also talk *with* the others affected by the incident. Of course, we must acknowledge that, for many students, past processes *haven't* been fair. Getting these students' investment in this new approach can take time. And it can take time for teachers to become comfortable with restorative practices, as well.

Teacher Samantha White suggests using restorative questions as part of a process to respond to a conflict or incident. *Restorative questions* focus on the situation; the expressions of thoughts, feelings, and effects of or on all persons involved; and ideas about how to restore the situation or make things right (White, 2012).

Knowing When and Whom to Ask for Help

Teachers don't always have to be the ones to solve every problem, particularly when 25 (or more) other students need their attention. If a student yells profanity at you, refuses to follow directions, won't get rid of their gum, or tells you what you can do and how you can do it, you, as the professional, usually have some discretion in how you choose to handle the situation. You don't have to win every time. However, you do want every situation to improve. Sometimes the best way to improve a situation—even when you feel you're in the right—is to seek help and support from someone else.

When you've tried everything and nothing seems to be working, **ask a colleague what to do.** Other teachers or administrators may be able to offer insight on the situation or approaches that have worked for them. You might explore whether a student's challenging behavior is widespread or limited to your classroom. If it's widespread, work with other staff members to create a consistent plan for dealing with the misbehavior. If it's limited to your class, examine your interactions with the student. Asking a colleague to observe you teaching might help you identify your role—if any—in causing the issue.

Talking with the school counselor or school psychologist can also be helpful. Counselors are a reservoir of ideas and have access to a wide range of resources. They are also good mediators and can help keep a conversation between you and the student on the right track. Take advantage of their specialized training and skills that can promote appropriate student behavior and help minimize disruptive behavior. And although we often think of school psychologists as living in the special education or testing realm, these trained mental health experts can effectively address school-related concerns, provide strategies for working with or instructing students, and help design plans to address behavioral problems.

Teachers—especially new teachers—sometimes hesitate to ask for help, believing that doing so will make them appear less than capable. There is truth in this. As school administrators, we both expected teachers to be on the front line of managing their classrooms. Teachers who constantly send misbehaving students to the office do not inspire confidence in students that they can handle difficult situations, and this can create additional problems. But any time a teacher came to talk with us about a difficult student and said, "I've tried *X, Y,* and *Z,* and nothing seems to work. I need help," we were there to provide the support needed.

Knowing When It's Not Your Decision

Then there's the *really* big stuff. We've never been fans of "zero-tolerance" policies, and many advocates for restorative justice promote it as an alternative to zero-tolerance policies and the harsh penalties that accompany them (Teasley, 2014). But there are some cases (e.g., weapon or drug possession, harassment or abuse, major fights) that truly cannot be tolerated. In these situations—ones that call for administrative, law enforcement, or legal involvement—avoid the temptation to try to resolve the issue yourself or otherwise bypass official policy. Let the appropriate designated authority take charge of the situation, with you participating if and as needed.

Having said that, we also realize that some school districts are harsh with punishment to the degree that teachers might hesitate to follow policy because they know the consequences for students can be truly life-altering. We encourage teachers who wish to take up the important work of disrupting the school-to-prison pipeline to have open conversations about this with decision makers in their district and to explore organized opportunities to eliminate discriminatory policies and change systems of harsh and biased punishment.

4

Belonging Thrives on Consistency

When teachers provide routines and consistency, it helps me know what to expect,
be prepared, stay on top of my work, and therefore have less anxiety about class.
an 11th grader

---

*This chapter highlights the importance of consistency—for you as a
teacher and for the students you serve. You'll be prompted to reevaluate
traditional classroom management practices through the lens of
promoting belonging and encounter strategies for establishing consistent
practices, protocols, and procedures; setting the behavioral tone;
clarifying directions; and establishing expectations for learning.*

As relationships, protocols, and expectations are established, students get a sense
of what it means to be a member of a particular class. It doesn't take long for each
one to begin to ask (and answer) the question "Do I belong?"

In the opening days of school and all the days beyond, students are watching
you. It may appear that they don't notice you exist, but do not be fooled: from the
beginning, and anew every day, students form impressions about whether they
can trust you to watch out for their emotional and physical safety. A major part of
that impression comes from how consistently you do what you say you will do and
how consistently you hold all students to expectations.

When schedules, procedures, expectations, and teacher behaviors are unpredictable and inconsistent, students may respond with anxiety, worry, stress, and

negative behaviors that exacerbate classroom management concerns. For students, knowing what to expect about the enforcement of classroom rules, how to ask questions, and even when they can leave class to go to the restroom is important. In addition, consistency in classroom logistics and operations—such as what the day's learning activities will be, what the assignments are and when they are due, and how a teacher "runs" a class—improves classroom management and goes a long way in promoting belonging.

Strategy 23: Treat Consistency as a Right

Consistency, consistency! You've heard this word hundreds of times. You've read the research about its importance, talked about it with colleagues, and probably agonized over whether you're delivering it for students. In their gut, all teachers know that they *must* follow through on what they've stated are the procedures and protocols in their classrooms. But so many of us have the hardest time doing it. We start each year with a fresh commitment to consistency; we promise ourselves we won't let it melt away. But then . . . it does. And we end up laden with regret and struggling with classroom management.

So what's the secret to providing consistency? How can you stick to the routines, expectations, and (particularly) the consequences that you have set out for your students? Here's how—and please notice that the *how* is intricately tied to the *why*.

To start, stop thinking of consistency as a chore. Actually, consistency isn't about thinking at all, and it isn't about making resolutions or having the grit and determination to keep them. Consistency is about honoring an obligation. It comes from the place where your deepest values lie. Most likely you became a teacher because you believe in kids and want to see them grow as human beings and learners. Here's the truth: you can't help students grow to be and do their best without consistency.

Treat consistency as your students' right. Be consistent because you care about them and because you know consistency is what they deserve and need.

There are a couple of cautionary notes to keep in mind. Don't establish a rule, procedure, or protocol that you do not believe yourself capable of consistently reinforcing, following through on, or holding students accountable for. But also understand that consistency doesn't mean rigidity. You must treat students *equitably,* which means letting go of the idea that there's a single right way to deal with each student and every situation. Consider your knowledge of each student and deal with the situation in the way that best meets that student's needs, the needs of the whole class, and your needs as well.

Predictable teacher behavior (in following procedures and responding to issues) helps to hold the group together. It deepens the sense of connection. A lack of it thwarts the very foundations of belonging. To belong, students need ongoing, stable acceptance and treatment they can count on. We want to take just a few more minutes to delve deeper into the *why* of consistency.

Consistency Promotes Safety and Builds Trust

To feel safe—physically, emotionally, and socially—students need to know what's coming next. Safety goes out the window when routines and consequences are unpredictable. It's undermined when stated norms seem fluid or expectations turn out to be randomly or selectively enforced. This makes students feel anxious. In turn, their sense of security takes a dive.

When a student watches a teacher respond to individual students differently without understanding why, apply expectations and consequences unevenly, or let routines slide, trust in the teacher erodes. Students lose respect for the teacher who doesn't follow through on commitments and procedures. A lack of consistency disrespects students and negatively affects classroom management.

Consistency Supports Equity and Fairness

Consistency means holding all students accountable for following the rules—and not letting bias or personal feelings sway you to be "tough" on some and "more lenient" with others. However, and as noted, it's essential to remember that your class is composed of unique individuals who possess unique personalities and are driven by different motivators. It most likely includes students with learning challenges or other disabilities, as well as students who have suffered trauma or discrimination. For these reasons, meeting each individual's inappropriate action with the exact same consequences may be "equal," but it's not always fair.

In your efforts to ensure equitable consistency, be sure to discuss with your class the question "Is *fair* always *equal?*" You want everyone to understand that you are committed to fairness, and understand why a classmate who might seem to be getting "special treatment" is instead getting the "fair" treatment she needs to be successful. For example, perhaps you have a student on the autism spectrum whom you permit to get up and pace in the back of the room during class because he needs the movement in order to be able to concentrate. You and your students might discuss why this may not be *equal* treatment but is *fair* treatment: "In our classroom, fairness means ensuring everyone gets what they need to succeed."

Consistency Encourages Self-Control, Diminishes Misbehavior, and Boosts Learning

Self-control allows a person to respond to situations appropriately, sometimes by overriding an impulse to do otherwise. Some of the greatest contributors to self-control are having guidelines, clear consequences, and good role models. Hit-or-miss, unpredictable, inequitably applied classroom management practically guarantees that some students will struggle to override impulses. They'll feel confused or easily swayed. Some will push limits to see what they can get away with.

Students learn best when consistent practices and accountability are the norm. A chaotic, unpredictable classroom climate interferes with every student's ability to succeed academically. A classroom that's free from regular disruptions frees students from worrying about being distracted, bothered, or belittled; they can more easily focus on their studies.

Consistency Bolsters Classroom Management

With consistency, everything in the classroom works better; everybody does better and has a better chance of thriving (the teacher included). Students treat one another with more kindness and respect. Overall, the group is more cohesive, and classroom life is more harmonious. Without consistency, your management plan will fall apart. Every slip in following the details will eat away at the climate you worked hard to establish. You'll be dissatisfied, frustrated—maybe even miserable. Students will suffer.

Uncertainty, lack of belonging, insecurity, anxiety, mistrust, betrayal, lack of respect, weakened self-control, diminished learning success, increased misbehavior and distractions—certainly, these are *not* the outcomes you intend for your students. But they can be the unintended results when a teacher does not follow through on the positive, effective details of classroom management.

Taking that to heart, honor your students by honoring their right to consistency. For many students, it will be a delightful surprise, because they're not used to adults following through. Yet this is what students need and want. Enjoy watching students and your classroom community flourish in response.

Strategy 24: Set the Behavioral Tone Early

Of all the factors in the classroom, behavior quite possibly has the strongest connection to belonging. Your expectations for behavior and the behaviors of every individual in your classroom play major roles in students' comfort, safety, and success. Students begin to get a sense of the behavioral "tone" in your classroom as early as the first day of school.

You begin to set the tone by letting students know what is expected of them. But the behavioral tone is most powerfully and memorably set by the example of how you behave toward them and by how you respond when the behavior pushes the limits of (or outright ignores) expectations. From that first day, students are watching to see how important those expectations really are, how (and if) they will be consistently enforced, and how (and if) you follow them yourself.

There are some simple, effective practices that can support any positive behavior system or codes of conduct you've planned for your students.

Treat Students with Equity, Respect, and Dignity

Even in cases of repeated or hostile misbehavior, be kind to all students. Fiercely protect their dignity. Show you believe in their value. As part of a respectful response, treat students fairly. Stay true to the expectations and consequences already outlined for students.

At the same time, regularly examine your own beliefs and practices to ensure you are treating every student in a fair and consistent manner and are not disproportionately disciplining students of color or other marginalized populations. Telling a student to look you in the eye when you are talking to her may be viewed as disrespectful in some cultures and respectful in others; it may be difficult for some students with disabilities or anxiety. Be aware that standards of "rudeness" and "honest feedback" may be culturally influenced as well. Do your homework, and find out about cultural practices, expectations, and mores so that you can do your very best to show respect for all cultures.

It's also important to be sensitive to gender identity and equality. Your students may identify as boys, girls, both, or neither—or they may not be sure.

Closely examine your own attitudes to identify any gender stereotypes or biases that you hold. Take care not to further stereotypes by what you expect or ask of boys and girls.

Model the Behaviors You Expect from Your Students

Constantly assess whether you treat your students in the way you want them to treat others. You've outlined protocols for your students; do they see those behaviors in you?

- Do you model respect and courtesy with simple phrases such as "please" and "thank you"?
- Do you treat colleagues and parents with the same respect you expect from students?
- Do you listen carefully when a student is talking to you (or are you trying to multitask)?
- Do you help students articulate their concerns and emotions through gentle questioning and paraphrasing?

Any response you give to misbehavior or any attempts you make to head off misbehavior affect not only the student involved but also the other students watching you. You may intend to talk with a student privately, but other students are bound to hear about what is happening and how you are handling things and relating to the student in question—even when the issue is fairly minor.

Accentuate the Positive and Use Humor as a Diffuser

Focus on recognizing students' positive actions more than watching for and punishing misbehavior. Remember, most students do the right thing most of the time. Look for and affirm students who are following protocols and guidelines.

A smile and a laugh can go a long way to minimize a potential problem or dispel tension. But be very cautious with sarcastic humor, which can backfire and exacerbate an issue.

Anticipate and Practice

As you get to know your students, think about the kinds of issues that may arise. Is there a student who wants to be the center of attention? Is there someone who is withdrawn and reluctant to participate? Are any students likely to be the target of discrimination, bullying, or unkind remarks by fellow students? What are *your* buttons that students may try to push? If you think through these issues ahead of time and imagine how different scenarios might occur, you can plan for and better position yourself to prevent problems and conflict. Decide ahead of time how best to react in a calm, reasonable manner that holds students accountable for their actions while continuing to build a community where everyone belongs.

Choose the Path of Least Resistance

What's the smallest action you can take to deal with a situation? Is it to ignore, minimize, give a "look," redirect the student by asking a question, or casually walk over and stand beside the student? Keep it as simple (and non–attention getting) as you can. Many problems are quieted or defused by simple teacher actions or presence. Your intervention should improve the situation, not make it worse. For example, Laurie remembers a situation in a school hallway where one student was playfully poking another. A teacher caught up with them, but instead of reprimanding the offending student, she began asking about his day. The student stopped poking the other student and, as a bonus, realized this teacher was interested in his life outside her classroom.

Keep Calm and Carry On

Never get caught up in arguments with students. We had a sign in our staff room that reminded everyone, "Arguing with a young adolescent is like wrestling with a pig. You both get dirty, but the pig loves it!" If you need to redirect or caution, do it calmly, quickly, and move on—without further disturbing the class. Be willing to remove yourself from the situation and have another adult assist if you feel you are getting too emotional and can no longer remain a calm, professional adult.

It's fine to take a few moments to compose yourself. If it's a tough situation and you just don't know what to do, or you're worried your own behavior might escalate, respond by saying something along the lines of "I'm very frustrated by this right now, but I need some time to think about it before we talk. See me after class, and we'll talk then."

Don't put on a show for the class, and don't blame, ridicule, or back a student into a corner. Public reprimands are demeaning. They create major setbacks to the student's trust in you and sense of belonging. In addition, public scolding can trigger a face-saving performance by the student (something you definitely want to avoid) and end up creating additional classroom management issues. A wise friend once gave us this advice: "Most students would rather be seen as disruptive than undignified. Don't give them an excuse to escalate their behavior based on your actions."

Adopt a Problem-Solving Mode

Remember that, in most cases, it's not about you.

Patti remembers a student who was sent to her office for yelling at a teacher. The student had dozed off in class, and the teacher sharply called him on it; he responded negatively, and the issue escalated. In talking with him, Patti learned that the student's mother's ex-boyfriend had come to their home in the middle of the night and broken in. He hit the student's mom, the police were called, and the ex-boyfriend was handcuffed and taken off to jail. Three hours later, the student reported to school and promptly fell asleep in class.

It's more effective to approach behavior issues in a problem-solving mode rather than from a need to blame or control. How different might things have been if this student's teacher had just let him sleep and then later quietly asked him if everything was OK or if he needed help? Showing students that you care about them and their problems goes a long way in building a relationship.

Watch Your Language

Don't label actions as "good" or "bad." Better choices include words such as *positive, helpful, acceptable, supportive, disruptive, distracting*, or *unacceptable*. And always distinguish between students and their behavior; remember, you are disapproving of their actions or behavior, not them personally. As with modeling the behaviors you want to see in your students, this sends the message "We can disagree and still be kind."

Remember What You Can Control

You can only control you.

Much of our success as teachers is built on how we work with students. There is a difference between being in charge and being in control. You can be in charge of a *situation*, but you cannot be in control of any *individual* but yourself.

When Laurie was a principal, her staff came to the agreement that they would limit interventions to positive action; unless someone's immediate safety was at risk, they would not intervene unless they were sure their action would improve a situation. If you have questions as to whether an action you're considering might make a situation worse, it can be wiser to wait and seek assistance from another adult.

Prioritize Relationship Building

In Chapter 2, we said that working on individual, trusting relationships with students is like putting money in the bank. Well, during the course of a year, it's likely that you will need to make withdrawals from some of those accounts. It definitely helps if there's already a relationship in place; otherwise, the bank account will be empty when you need it most.

Patti vividly remembers when she was a fairly new assistant principal in charge of overseeing school discipline. Randy, a student with "high-level frequent flyer status," was waiting to see her in the area outside her office. A parent was walking by in the hall, saw Patti standing in the office, walked right in, and started loudly complaining about how Patti had handled an incident with her son. She was very worked up, using profanity, and making rather unflattering allegations about Patti's character. Another adult in the office asked Randy, who was sitting and watching all of this happen, to step out of the office with her. Later, when the parent had calmed down and left and Randy had returned to class, the staff member told Patti that Randy's first remarks were "That lady doesn't know what she's talking about! Mrs. Kinney would never treat anyone that way." Remember, Randy was a student Patti saw on a regular basis for discipline-related reasons. The power of a relationship won again.

Strategy 25: Develop and Teach Clear Procedures and Protocols

It's a familiar theme in this book: predictable and consistent procedures and protocols for classroom management and belonging are a critical part of classroom management. To succeed academically and socially, and to belong, students need sensible, doable routines and expectations. They need a structure that provides freedom from disorganization, uncertainty, and constant changes. With consistent routines, students are more likely to see themselves as part of the group rather than lone figures, floundering and trying to decide what to do next.

Procedures are the frequent (often daily or many times daily) tasks, practices, and activities of a classroom. *Protocols* are guidelines for behavior in general and behavior in particular situations. This strategy incorporates some suggestions for setting and maintaining practices that provide the reliability and consistency for classroom life and relationships—expanding on the *why* and *how* of consistency that we discussed in Strategy 23.

Set Procedures and Protocols

Honor schoolwide practices. Because school procedures and practices are meant for everyone in the school to follow, design your classroom guidelines to support school-level decisions. It defeats the purpose and is extremely frustrating to introduce a schoolwide practice only to hear your students protest, "Mr. Jones said we're going to do it differently in his class!" Most schools have schoolwide protocols to promote safety, and many also follow an established discipline policy or positive behavioral support program.

Plan ahead. Whatever terms you use for everyday practices and expectations, don't start classroom life without defining them clearly. When students are confused or don't understand how they are supposed to proceed, the classroom can become chaotic and very challenging to manage. Consider what procedures will be necessary for your class to operate in a smooth manner. Choose your list, but don't stop there. Think through every procedure carefully. Write it down. Know why students must do it. Envision how it will work. Identify the details.

Identify the procedures you and your students will follow and the protocols you will consistently promote. In your classroom, you will need defined procedures for a variety of situations throughout the school day (see Figure 4.1), and defined protocols (guidelines, expectations, and consequences) for actions (or inactions) related to

- Interacting with others in the classroom and the school;
- Managing personal time, behavior (including verbal behavior), and emotions; and
- Being responsible for one's own choices and actions.

Include students in the choices and design of procedures and protocols. Chances are, you start the school year with classroom procedures firmly in your mind. But remember, it's the students' classroom, too—and they are more

FIGURE 4.1

Classroom Situations That Require Procedures

Situation	Examples of Procedures to Establish
Starting and ending class	How to enter the room How to enter the room when arriving late How to tackle "bell starter" and "exit ticket" activities
Moving around the classroom	How approach restroom/drinking fountain permissions How to retrieve and store supplies and necessities (such as tissues) How to dispose of trash
Interacting with the teacher/paraprofessionals	How to ask questions How and whom to ask for help How to signal for attention
Interacting with classmates	How to work together in pairs or other small groups How to give supportive feedback How to resolve conflict/misunderstandings
Managing classwork	How to keep track of assignments How to spend your time when you finish assigned work early How to turn in work (including homework) How to make up missed assignments
Venturing outside the classroom	How to move through the school as a group How to behave during assemblies How to use the library, science lab, or other out-of-classroom space
Managing technology	How to use computers, other devices, and the internet for assignments How to handle cell phones in class (e.g., using/not using or storing out of sight, dependent upon schoolwide protocols)

likely to feel committed to and honor procedures and expectations that they have been trusted to help design. As you get ready to put procedures into practice, make student participation part of the process. You'll be honoring students' opinions while at the same time contributing to increased belonging for all students.

At just about all ages, students are capable of and should be involved in identifying needed procedures and planning some of the details. Students can work in pairs or small groups to identify procedures that are needed or practices that have worked well before. Or give groups the task of working out details of some specific classroom practices. Students can also take part in the process of teaching procedures. Once you've modeled the process for a few procedures, they'll know how to do it.

If you teach multiple sections, begin with a list you have already developed and allow each class period to offer input and ideas. In doing this, you retain some much-needed consistency from class period to class period, while also honoring specific input from each group of students.

Teach—Don't Preach—the Protocols and Procedures

Wouldn't it be nice if we could present and explain procedures once and students would remember and follow them for the remainder of the school year? Let's get real: it's not going to happen. Students will forget or push the limits—even (or especially) the older ones. Whether a procedure is schoolwide or classroom-specific, think of it as *content*. All content needs to be taught in context and taught and retaught so that it's mastered by all.

Present procedures at the right time. When the year starts, it's easy to get swallowed up in describing and establishing all the many ways things will be done. Although it is necessary to have a secure, orderly environment for learning, trying to teach and practice all expectations at once is mind-boggling. Introduce your classroom practices (procedures) and expectations (protocols) gradually and thoughtfully—and preferably, in context.

Teach specific procedures when they are needed. For example, teach assembly procedures and expectations a few days before the first assembly. If you focus on that topic the first day of school and there's no assembly for three weeks, you've wasted everybody's time. Be sure to allow enough advance time for stating, reviewing, and practicing the procedure.

Make every procedure clear. Teaching a procedure begins with stating what it is. Don't start until you know what you'll say. You don't want to get partway through the directions and then realize you missed a critical piece and have to start over; in backtracking, you'll probably lose two-thirds of the class. Write out your procedures so you'll be confident about what you will say. Make each one a clear, brief statement. Make the statement twice. An example might be "When I need your attention, I will raise my arm." And then you might restate the exact same words again: "When I need your attention, I will raise my arm." Or you might rephrase the statement just a bit, to something like "Again, if my arm is in the air, I need your attention."

Give necessary details. Students who don't understand what they are supposed to do can get confused and anxious. This might happen when you simply state an expected behavior without providing pertinent details. What, exactly, are you asking a student to do? Know what you want, and communicate it. For example, you might tell your students, "When I raise my arms in the air, I expect you to do all of the following . . .

- "Look at me."
- "Raise one of your arms."
- "Stop in place."
- "Stop talking."
- "Stop everything you are doing."
- "Listen until I tell you to put your arm down."
- "Follow the directions I will then give."

Provide a reason for the protocols and procedures. Students will be more willing to follow a procedure if they understand why it was created. Discuss the rationale behind it; allow students to ask questions and suggest modifications to improve the process. You can even ask a group of students to model what happens when the procedure is followed and another group to demonstrate what happens if it is not. Knowing they have a real part in designing processes and procedures for their classroom is a big boost to all students' sense of belonging (and subsequent behavior) in your class.

Launch with intention. Show students the behavior you're looking for. Get them involved in demonstrating and role-playing procedures and protocols. When they do this, it provides you with an opportunity to restate the key points or emphasize expected behaviors.

Practice, practice, practice. Teaching class procedures and protocols is a yearlong process. Don't let this process dwindle away and disappear. Any procedure or protocol worthy of putting on your list is important enough to review (many times). They're key to living together in a smoothly operating, belonging-centered classroom. To ensure they continue throughout the school year, we recommend you

- Have students make posters that define specific procedures and display these in the classroom.
- Put into writing any procedures or expectations that are complex. For example, when expecting a classroom visitor, write a note to each student

describing the details and expected behaviors, or list these on the board for all to see.

- Regularly check to see that all students understand the practices. A good time to review procedures and protocols is when students have been out of school for a while, such as after a holiday or spring break.

Students who learn a procedure or protocol by doing it together, correctly and repeatedly, gain comfort with it as a normal part of classroom life. This comfort translates into belonging—a feeling that "we are all learning and practicing this together and helping one another"—and into a better-managed classroom as well.

Strategy 26: Give Clear and Concise Directions

Do you find yourself repeating instructions to your students over and over (and over) and thinking, "Why can't they follow my directions"? When you feel this frustration—stop. Take a breath. When a student says, "I don't get it" or asks, "What are we supposed to do?" it's not always the student's fault. Consistently giving clear directions for activities and assignments is a fundamental skill of instruction that directly affects classroom management. That skill includes giving clear and concise directions and checking for students' understanding of those directions.

When directions are unclear, it's hard for students to move forward and succeed. Unsure of what to do, some students slip into doing nothing or distracting others. Classroom order suffers. The learning climate becomes unfocused, even chaotic. Students who are unsure of what to do can feel lost, detached from the group. That feeling of "everybody else knows what to do, but *I* don't" lessens the student's sense of belonging and increases classroom management issues.

So how can you better ensure that your directions will be understandable and promote a calmer classroom?

Clarify What You Want

Are you absolutely clear about your goals for a given activity or lesson? Consider these questions:

- What is the task's goal?
- What is its purpose?
- Why is this an important task for students?

- What is the intended outcome?
- What, exactly, am I asking of them?

Have you carefully thought through just what it will take for your students to follow the instructions? Consider these questions:

- How many different things must students remember to do?
- Am I asking them to do anything that might be new to them?
- Are they capable of doing everything without help?
- Is it important they follow a specific sequence, or do they have some choice in approaching the assignment?
- Should the directions be written, verbal, visual, or a combination of these? Do I have students with learning challenges or for whom English is a second language who might need additional supports to understand the instructions?
- What tasks (and how many steps) will be involved in following the directions? For example, "Let's get ready to go to the library" is a much more complex direction than "Take out a pencil and paper."

Unless the directions are very simple and brief, write them down for yourself.

Make Your Delivery Effective

Once you are certain of what you will say, take care to deliver your directions in a deliberate way.

Get students' attention. Use whatever attention-getting signal the class has practiced. Don't start giving directions while students are working on something else. If you start to give directions without being certain that everyone is listening, the students (and you) will be set up for failure.

Present your directions. Not too many at a time—three is good; use fewer if it's new material. Then check to see that the directions are understood: "Raise your hand if you know what to do first" or "What are the three things you have to do?" Randomly ask students to state what to do first, second, or third, or to repeat all the directions.

Model what is expected, and give students time to master the procedure. Modeling is especially important for new or complex procedures and routines. Following the gradual release of responsibility model works as well when it's applied to master a complicated task or set of procedural instructions as it does when applied to understand new content and develop new skills:

I (teacher) model the process first.

Then **we** (teacher and students) carry out the process together, with teacher guidance.

Then **you** (students) practice carrying out the process together, perhaps through role-play.

Finally, **you** (individual student) carry out the process independently.

When carrying out the process requires movement throughout the classroom, decide ahead of time if everyone should move at the same time or in groups. Monitor what is happening, and help students when necessary.

Determine if reteaching or remediation is needed. Do you need to work with a few struggling students? If a few days or weeks go by and the procedure proves ineffective or less effective than you'd like, how might you revise or rethink the procedure?

Strategy 27: Post a Daily Agenda

Because the goals of your lessons should be about what students are to learn and do, your students need to know what those goals are. When students are "lost in class" because they didn't "get" all of the verbal explanations or when a student didn't hear or doesn't remember what is happening next, this is a threat to safety and belongingness. Further, feelings of confusion and uncertainty are often the seeds of management issues.

Consistently write your daily plan on the board for students to see, in words that they understand. Posting a simple, easy-to-read lesson plan in an area visible to all students for the entire class period is more helpful than having it scroll on an interactive whiteboard and disappear five minutes into the lesson. A daily agenda is a useful organizational and classroom management tool, and it is a good learning tool. We suggest posting the following every day:

1. The date
2. The content standard related to the day's lesson—not just the label but the actual complete standard, rephrased as necessary in student-friendly language

3. An essential question about the content standard that will be answered within the lesson
4. The agenda—a summary of the day's lesson plan that students can understand, describing what will happen without the details as to how
5. Upcoming assignments, tests, due dates, class events, and school events

Using this approach, you are far less likely to hear questions like "What's today's date?" "Are we doing anything today?" "Why do we have to learn this?" "Do we have homework?" or "When's the test on this?"

Students have good reason to want these questions answered. But you'll have a management problem on your hands if they pepper you for answers throughout class time. It's all about consistency; students will learn early on that this information will be available to them in plain sight, every day, throughout the class. The agenda-posting practice boosts security, individual responsibility, and confidence. It increases comfort and, with it, a sense of belonging. Because no student has to flounder around wondering what to do, everyone can focus their brains on the lessons! Figure 4.2 offers some sample daily agendas for a different age levels and content areas.

Notice that, in all of these examples, the daily agenda doesn't list any instructional strategies. If reading in pairs didn't work out in 2nd period, you're not stuck

---

FIGURE 4.2

Sample Daily Agendas

Agenda for a 2nd grade math class	
Date	Tuesday, May 4, 2021
Standard	I can count within 1,000 and skip-count by 5s, 10s, and 100s.
Essential question	How do you count by 10s to 200?
Daily agenda	1. Complete bell ringer activity 2. Review counting by 5s 3. Counting by 10s activity 4. Answer essential question
Upcoming	1. TEST on counting by 5s, 10s, and 100s on **Friday, May 7** 2. Field Day on **Friday, May 14**

Agenda for a 6th grade science class	
Date	Tuesday, May 4, 2021
Standard	I know how to collect data to provide evidence for how the motions and complex interactions of air masses result in changes in weather conditions.
Essential question	What causes sudden changes in weather?
Daily agenda	1. Complete bell ringer activity 2. Review and discuss temperature, pressure, humidity, precipitation, and wind 3. Air masses diagram 4. Prep for condensation lab 5. Answer essential question
Upcoming	1. Condensation lab on **Wednesday, May 5** 2. Quiz on air masses on **Friday, May 7** 3. Weather and climate test on **Tuesday, May 11**
Agenda for a 10th grade English class	
Date	Tuesday, May 4, 2021
Standard	I can cite strong and thorough textual evidence to support analysis of what the text says explicitly as well as inferences drawn from the text.
Essential question	How do you prove a claim in literature?
Daily agenda	1. Complete bell ringer activity 2. Review and discuss Chapter 2 of *A Tale of Two Cities* 3. Read and discuss Chapter 3 of *A Tale of Two Cities* 4. Make a claim and cite evidence to support analysis of text 5. Answer essential question
Upcoming	1. Quiz on *A Tale of Two Cities* Chapters 1–3 on **Friday, May 7** (*Hint:* Be prepared to make and support a claim!) 2. Pep rally/abbreviated schedule on **Tuesday, May 11** 3. Compare/contrast essay on *A Tale of Two Cities* due on **Friday, May 14**

Note: List the actual number of the standard only if you want to list it or your school requires it; students don't need these labels. Students benefit from understanding what they are expected to know and be able to do. In that spirit, it is also helpful if you can reword the standard into "I" statements that students can understand and relate to, which these examples do.

with it in 4th period. If cooperative learning worked great in 2nd period but you're a little worried about your 5th period, you can change it up based on class needs. Your agenda is simply giving students a picture of what the day or period will look like. Save the instructional strategy details for when you get to each step of the lesson plan.

Strategy 28: Start with a Spark, End with a Bang

The beginning of class, the end of class, and transitions between activities are prime times for brief but powerfully positive or negative "hits" on classroom harmony, management, and feelings of belonging. As such, it's wise to create specific routines, traditions, and expectations for these portions of class time.

Establish Beginning-of-Class Routines

You can help all students enter class without anxiety or threats to their sense of belonging by ensuring they know what to expect and what to do. We recommend greeting students as they walk in the door and providing something for them to do before the bell, while you continue greeting their arriving classmates.

These "class starters" can be a daily question, task, or activity that students can complete on their own with little help from others. Starters can be written or projected on the board, on a half-sheet of paper handed to students as they enter the classroom ("entry tickets"), or sent electronically in advance. Class starters can be a great activating strategy to review content from your previous lesson, help focus students on learning to come, and decrease the likelihood of classroom disruptions.

If there is no structured task, students will begin to use the time as they choose (which may present obstacles to belonging as students possibly pair up, leave some classmates out, etc.), and you will need to spend time gathering and focusing the class after you greet your final student entering the class that day, cutting into your instructional time.

Plan for Transitions

With creative planning and direction, the time between activities can give students a break for stretching, moving, and refreshing their brains—without chances for disruptive behavior and unwanted classroom management concerns. If you make positive use of this time, students will be eager for the next event and ready to get to work. Here are some things to think about when planning for transitions:

- Establishing transition routines
- Ensuring continuation of classroom protocols through transition times and classroom traditions
- Signaling transitions
- Whether to transition as a group (everyone back to their seats at once), in small groups (Groups 1 and 2 go back to their seats first, followed by Groups 3 and 4), or individually (go back your seat after you complete a specific task)

Establish End-of-Class Routines

Aim to help all students leave class each day without anxiety, knowing what they'll need to do to prepare for the next day and feeling a sense of accomplishment and belonging.

There are many elements to successfully closing a class each day. Establishing a routine for this process can be very helpful to students. For example, you may want to begin wrapping up class at a certain time before class dismissal each day (e.g., announcing a five-minute countdown, allowing one minute to gather belongings and chat with friends, redirecting students to homework).

Consider end-of-class routines that serve as formative assessment. For example, if you've posted an essential question for the content lesson for the day, set this as an "exit ticket," and ask students to answer the question before they leave via electronic communication, a notecard they turn in, or a verbal answer on the way out the door. Then use their responses to inform your instructional plans (including differentiation, as needed) for the next day's lesson.

These same strategies can be used with questions that focus on a student's well-being, sense of belonging, effort given, or assessment of behavior. You might also employ more informal methods (such as thumbs up/thumbs down), direct students to self-assessment questions from a posted list, or ask them to submit questions to you.

Strategy 29: Design Guidelines for Classroom Conversations

"We care about one another" should be a thread that consistently runs through all classrooms. Appropriate classroom conversations—how the teacher speaks to students, how students speak to the teacher, and how students speak to one another—are one of the greatest indicators of a culture that promotes belonging and minimizes behavioral issues. But it's good to have some established guidelines that remind everyone of their responsibility in building an environment that supports all individuals, their beliefs, and their dignity. In order to feel safe in a classroom, students must know that they can participate safely.

As an example, we present a set of guidelines Patti used at the school level. You can use it as a template or share it as inspiration for your students as your class or school creates their own guidelines for conversations. Students can work together or in small groups to illustrate these points (or the ones they create to use as guidelines) on posters to hang on classroom walls or school hallways. As a bonus, this set of guidelines comes with an easy-to-remember acronym: "We CARE."

The *C* is for "communicate." As a class, discuss appropriate "rules" for communication that ensure conversations are positive, polite, and productive. Consider sharing the Rotary Four-Way Test for "things we think, say, or do" (Rotary, 2020). According to Rotary's foundational principles, members are encouraged to ask this of everything they think, say, or do when working together.

- Is it the truth?
- Is it fair to all concerned?
- Will it build goodwill and better friendships?
- Will it be beneficial to all concerned?

Although this protocol was written for adults collaborating in a professional setting, it can serve as a starting point for your classroom conversation about communication.

The *A* is for "appreciate." Students don't always know (or remember to use) words that show appreciation. Here's a list to get your class started on creating their own list of words that show appreciation—feel free to swap in current slang for saying "thanks," "you're the best," and so on:

- Thank you.
- I appreciate you.
- I am grateful.
- You're so thoughtful.
- What a friendly action that was.
- I'm honored that you thought to do that.
- This is great.
- My sincere thanks.
- You're the best.
- You've been very helpful.

The *R* is for "respect." *Respect* can be defined as feeling or showing regard for the feelings, wishes, rights, or traditions of someone or something. Examples of respect are being quiet in church, truly listening to someone speak, or finding a garbage can to throw away your trash. Work with your students to create your own examples or list of ways to show respect in the classroom. Here are a few to get you started:

- **Listen.** Truly listening to what another person has to say is a basic way to respect them.
- **Support.** When we support someone, we're giving evidence that they matter.
- **Serve.** Helping out when not asked to do so is an unexpected way to show respect.
- **Be kind.** When someone is having a bad day, being kind instead of making fun shows respect.
- **Be polite.** Letting someone go ahead of you in the lunch line is a way to be polite.
- **Be thankful.** Saying "thank you" when someone helps you shows respect.
- **Be inclusive.** Welcome students who speak different languages, come from other cultures, have physical or learning differences, are of different races and ethnicities, and so on.

The *E* is for "encourage." Mother Teresa is often credited with saying, "Kind words can be short and easy to speak, but their echoes are truly endless." This is true for words of encouragement. You can help your students articulate ways they encourage their classmates—and take note of what they say and use those words for giving encouragement, yourself. Here are a few to get you started:

- Hang in there.
- Don't give up.
- Keep pushing.
- Keep fighting!
- Stay strong.
- Never give up.
- Never say "never."
- Come on! You can do it!
- I believe in you!

5

Belonging Thrives on Social and Emotional Competence

The better I get to know my classmates, the more I feel I belong.

an 8th grader

This chapter includes strategies for building personal social and emotional skills within the context of the classroom group. These strategies are designed to help students learn and practice skills such as goal setting and accomplishment, self-management, active listening, increasing their own belonging and the belongingness of others, perspective taking, and conflict resolution. It's important to note that many of these strategies can be integrated into content-based lessons, regardless of the subject matter.

Researchers who study the topic of belonging conclude that the intentional teaching of specific social and emotional skills has a positive influence on a student's sense of belonging in the classroom and school (U.S. Centers for Disease Control and Prevention, 2009; Wingspread, 2004). An even broader body of research stretches beyond belonging to identify numerous benefits of teaching social and emotional skills. In a meta-analysis of over 200 social and emotional learning (SEL) programs, SEL was associated with increased academic performance, stronger positive relationships with peers, reduced misbehavior, and less anxiety (Durlak, Weissberg, Dymnicki, Taylor, & Schellinger, 2011). A more recent review of SEL programs found that they contribute to positive behavior, reduce emotional distress, and reduce misconduct (Dusenbury & Weissberg, 2017).

The Collaborative for Academic, Social, and Emotional Learning (CASEL) defines *social and emotional learning* as

> the process through which children and adults acquire and effectively apply the knowledge, attitudes, and skills necessary to understand and manage emotions, set and achieve positive goals, feel and show empathy for others, establish and maintain positive relationships, and make responsible decisions. (2020b)

CASEL's framework (2020a) identifies the five core SEL competencies as self-awareness, self-management, social awareness, relationship skills, and responsible decision making.

Social and emotional needs and expressions are at the core of every individual, including students and teachers. Throughout the school day, the social and emotional competencies of each individual in the classroom affect classroom life, classroom management, conditions for learning, and each student's sense of belonging. Intentional attention to developing these skills in ourselves and our students is just smart teaching.

Strategy 30: Begin the Belonging Conversation

It's better to demonstrate a commitment through action than to promise it with words alone. As essential as it is to deliberately communicate to students the message that they belong, we don't recommend making a big speech about belonging on the first day of school. Focus instead on setting the classroom climate, including the academic climate, in ways that welcome and include all students (see Strategy 6: Cultivate Belonging from Day 1 in Chapter 1 for suggestions). Then, a few weeks into the year or semester, begin a conversation that will wend its way through the rest of the year.

The Belonging Survey

This activity will help you begin a dialogue about belonging. The few minutes it takes will more than justify itself. In Chapter 2, we recommend surveying students to better understand how they believe teachers' actions or behaviors affect their sense of acceptance and belonging (see p. 30). A belonging survey can build on that information by gathering information on students' perceptions of school-wide belonging.

Write or project the word *belonging* at the front of the classroom. Tell students that the class will be taking some time to think about this idea, and distribute copies of a survey that's similar to what you see in Figure 5.1 but adapted to suit your students and information needs. Encourage them to be very thoughtful and honest, and give them space and time to reflect on the topic and record their responses. While students are completing their surveys, you should do so, too.

FIGURE 5.1

Student Survey on Schoolwide Belonging

Instructions: Think of each question as it relates to school. Answer as many as you can. Don't include your name or any student or teacher names.

1. What does it mean to "belong" in your school and your classes?

2. Why does it matter for students to feel a sense of belonging at school?

3. How can you tell if someone does NOT have a sense of belonging at school?

4. How do you think it feels to NOT have a sense of belonging at school?

5. What can teachers do to help students belong?

6. What can students do to help other students belong?

7. What is something you've done to help someone else belong?

8. What is something you could do to increase your own sense of belonging?

Source: From *Middle School: A Place to Belong and Become* (p. 243), by L. Barron and P. Kinney, 2018, Columbus, OH: AMLE. Copyright 2018 by AMLE. Adapted with permssion.

A belonging survey can help you to understand what your students see and feel about belonging and why it matters. In addition, you'll get some good ideas from the actions they describe. It'll be up to you implement these actions.

For your students, this survey experience inspires further engagement with the concept. You can build on what the students and you have learned from doing this. Remember that just the act of *thinking* about belonging or not belonging and the effects of either helps the state of belongingness in your classroom.

Belonging Dialogues

Soon after doing the survey, assign students to small groups to discuss some of these ideas. Make this a semi-guided exploration. Ask them to share and write down their ideas about increasing belonging by responding to questions like these:

- Why does belonging at school matter?
- What can be done (by students, by teachers) to try to see that everybody belongs in this classroom?
- What actions and words should be avoided to help others belong?
- How can we all increase our own sense of belonging?
- When have you felt that you didn't belong or were treated unjustly in school in the past?
- Are there ways our school community makes you feel you don't belong?
- What discrimination have you experienced or witnessed other students experience at school in the past?
- What steps can we take to recognize and address that discrimination and make sure that we all feel that we belong?

As part of guiding students' reflection, encourage them to think not only about behaviors but also about classroom and school practices, procedures, policies, and organization that might affect students' sense of belonging. Your students should feel safe and comfortable sharing all their thoughts and ideas, even those that might be tough to talk about. Until all the issues can be identified, it's difficult to find ways to solve the problems.

Belonging Recommendations

Ask small groups to agree on five key recommendations for what can be done (by students and by the teacher) to increase belonging. Ask them to include actions to do and to avoid and at least one recommendation of something students can do as individuals to increase their own belonging.

Find time for each group to share recommendations with the whole class. Record these for all to see. Ask all students to share their observations about the recommendations.

Belonging Actions

Finally, work on a consensus of four or five actions everyone will agree to put into practice in an effort to help everyone feel a greater sense of belonging. Discuss how these actions will affect classroom learning, atmosphere, and behavior. (If it seems appropriate, you might also share some of the research on the effects of belonging with your students.) Settle on a process for revisiting the topic and for reflecting on their recommendations and actions.

Strategy 31: Teach Skills That Increase Belonging

This book's Introduction includes an overview of some circumstances and factors that contribute to increasing students' senses of belonging. Here we will take a closer look at skills students can practice—specific skills and repeated practices that are shown to help increase their belonging. Always keep in mind that promoting belonging will positively affect your classroom management.

Read the list in Figure 5.2 thoughtfully, and keep it close at hand throughout the school year. Let it serve both as a reminder and topic guide for minilessons, attitudes, and behaviors to incorporate into your teaching. All of the described behaviors are critical SEL competencies. All of them, when learned and practiced—even in their beginning stages—contribute to effective classroom management and heightened belonging for students. In addition, most can readily become part of an academic experience in the classroom; they do not have to be approached in a separate lesson.

FIGURE 5.2
Log of Teachable Skills and Practices That Increase Belonging

The following skills and practices have been shown to increase belonging for students—on both the giving and receiving ends of the actions. Intentionally integrate these practices into your plans for lessons and activities. Indicate the dates that you provided an opportunity for your students to specifically practice each of the skills and what activities or lessons you presented.

Skill or Practice	Date	Lesson/Activity Notes
Give and expect respect from classmates		
Create an inclusive classroom community by embracing diversity (racial, linguistic, cultural, etc.) and engaging with differences with curiosity and respect		
Actively resist and protect against the exclusion of anyone		
Practice kindness and helpfulness		
Work collaboratively in diverse teams to complete tasks, make decisions, debate constructively, and solve problems— academic topics, classroom-living topics, and social issues in the local community		
Take some responsibility for their own belonging		

(continued)

FIGURE 5.2

Log of Teachable Skills and Practices That Increase Belonging (*continued*)

The following skills and practices have been shown to increase belonging for students—on both the giving and receiving ends of the actions. Intentionally integrate these practices into your plans for lessons and activities. Indicate the dates that you provided an opportunity for your students to specifically practice each of the skills and what activities or lessons you presented.

Skill or Practice	Date	Lesson/Activity Notes
Increase awareness and use of their own personal resources, skills, and abilities		
Increase social awareness in their communities and the wider world		
Grow in self-management and control of emotions in socially aware and meaningful ways that respect and honor differences		
Learn and practice organizational and planning skills		
Make choices about classroom life and their own learning		
Have a voice in classroom life and their own learning, and make efforts to hear from students who haven't had a voice		
Learn, practice, and improve skills of coping and flexibility		
Take part in making real and meaningful decisions		
Build self-awareness skills, including how they may relate to identity and equity		
Build reflection skills that help them "check in" with themselves in terms of their assumptions about the world and identify any biases that they have or may be developing		
Gain academic confidence and a satisfying view of themselves as students		
Experience mastery and competence		
Have experience with autonomy		
Set, manage, and achieve goals		
Learn ways to bounce back from failure		
Engage actively in learning activities		
Enjoy learning and opportunities to make it relevant to their lives and interests		
Enjoy fun, humor, and excitement in the classroom		
Have meaningful and frequent participation in classroom events of all sorts		
Participate in creative endeavors, leadership, and responsibility		
Advocate for themselves as learners and for issues they believe in, and seek help when needed		
Give and receive kind, constructive feedback		
Learn about and practice growth mindset		

As you make lesson plans for the content you teach, commit to including activities, attitudes, and strategies that offer explicit training for items from the list in Figure 5.2. You should be incorporating at least three experiences from the list every week. Choose and polish activities that have worked successfully with your students before, select strategies from this book, or glean ideas from colleagues or other resources.

Use the lesson/activity notes and date columns to record an experience. Remember that students need repeated experiences in all of these categories.

Strategy 32: Listen Carefully and Actively

As illustrated by the Telephone game—where one person whispers a sentence to the next person, who whispers it to the next person, and so on down the line until the message is completely muddled—there is often a world of difference between what one person says and what another person hears.

Active and careful listening is a critical skill for students to develop. It's just as crucial for adults, and students are unlikely to learn it well if the adults around them don't practice it. When what students are saying is actually heard, a sense of belonging is promoted; when students truly hear what others are saying, disagreements and arguments are averted. In today's world, with its emphasis on social media, owning the latest device, and lots of screen time, students may be more likely to withdraw from face-to-face conversations and only partially hear what is being said. And that can lead to classroom management problems.

Do You Hear What I Hear?

Large-group activities can help develop listening skills. While both the examples that follow may seem more appropriate for younger students, we've had good experiences using them with older students as well. It's all in the presentation; if you're having fun with it, students generally follow suit.

Simon Says. This classic game asks students to listen carefully to be sure that they only follow the directions that are preceded by the phrase "Simon says . . . ."

Can You Draw This? Give each student a blank piece of paper, and give a precise, concise drawing instruction, such as "Draw a circle in the upper middle of the paper." Students pass their paper to the next person, and you give another instruction: "Draw a star to the right of the circle." Once again, the paper is passed, and another instruction is given. When each student's original paper makes its way back to them (or when you've finished a sufficient number of steps to complete a picture), share the image of the picture you described—and have students compare this to their own and other students' renderings. How many were able to have it turn out close to the original?

For a variation of this, select an image that's unusual, and provide directions that are a little bit ambiguous or open to interpretation. Students don't pass their papers; they simply follow your instructions. For example, you might say,

> The body is a big oval in the middle of the page. The head is on the left side of the body and is one-third the size of the body. All four legs are showing. The tail is very curly. The pig is wearing orange tennis shoes. Its front legs are red, and its back legs are blue. The pig has two blue eyes and long eyelashes. Both ears are showing. There is a big pink spot on the upper end of the pig's body.

Give students one direction at a time, pausing while they draw. When you're finished, ask students to share and compare their drawings with the original image.

If You're Listening Well, It Shows

Work with students to design a strategy for active listening. Coming up with an acronym that can be used in a reminder poster can be a fun activity. It may look something like the one below. In this one, the word is *PLEASE*:

Posture. Sit up straight and be as close to the speaker as appropriate.

Listen. Hear with ears, eyes, brain, and heart.

Engage. Ask and answer questions.

Assure. Nod your head or give a similar action to show you are listening.

Shush. Don't interrupt the speaker.

Eye contact. Focus on the speaker, and don't let your eyes wander.

Yes, *but* . . . Yes, *and* . . .

Break up the class into pairs of students; in each pair, they decide who will be Student A and Student B. Review the class definition (from the preceding activity) of what active listening looks like.

Round 1. Tell students they are going to plan a class party.

To begin, Student A gives a suggestion (e.g., "I think we should have a pizza party"). Student B counters with, "Yes, *but* . . . ," giving an explanation as to why the suggestion won't work ("Yes, *but* there are a lot of students who'd rather have tacos"). Student A then responds with "Yes, *but* . . . ," to offer evidence for the suggestion's efficacy ("Yes, *but* we could order a few taco pizzas"). This process goes back and forth for a few minutes and requires each student to carefully hear what the other is saying in order to rebut it.

Round 2. Still planning the party in the same pairs, it's Student B's turn to offer a suggestion (e.g., "I think we should have dancing at the party"). This time, Student A responds with "Yes, *and* . . . ," ("Yes, *and* I have a friend who's a DJ, and I bet we could get him to come!"), building on the suggestion with additional ideas. Student A responds with "Yes, *and* . . . ," and the conversation continues in this manner for a few minutes. Again, students must listen to each other's responses in order to build upon what is being said.

Debrief. This process can also lead into a great discussion about collaboration and cooperation. Ask students to respond to the following questions:

- What was easy and what was hard about listening to each other? Why?
- What was the difference between using "Yes, *but* . . . " and "Yes, *and* . . ."?
- Which answer do you think led to a better solution for the task you were given and why?

Throughout this activity, make sure that all students have an equally active voice and participate, especially those who tend to keep their thoughts to themselves. This idea can also be used for a discussion of class content, but bear in mind that it will work best in subject areas that lend themselves to opinions rather than facts—literature, social studies, and so on.

Strategy 33: Help Students Develop and Reach Goals

When students successfully set, pursue, and accomplish goals, their confidence, independence, and competence soar. Teach and practice a process for following one's goals. This strategy can be especially helpful for students when taught at the beginning or end of a grading period or as a part of student-led conferences. Remember that a "goal" may be behavioral as well as academic.

1. Brainstorm and discuss goals that students want to accomplish. As a part of the discussion, help them understand that goals must be SMARRT:

   Specific—stated clearly

   Measurable—stated in terms of what they will *do;* someone else can come along and see whether the goal was accomplished

   Attainable—something that is within their abilities to do

   Relevant—something that is culturally affirming, meaningful, or useful for them to learn, that applies to their life, and that is important enough to commit time to doing

   Realistic—something that is actually doable with the time and resources they have available

   Time-sensitive—something that can be finished in the amount of time available

2. Assist students in making action plans. This process includes task analysis and breaking down the goal into small steps. You might assist students with devising a graphic organizer or adapting the goal-setting template in Figure 5.3.

FIGURE 5.3

Template for Student Goal Setting

NAME:		
GOAL:		
What I need to learn, practice, or be able to do:		
Resources I can use:		
Where I can get help (or from whom):		
THE PLAN:		

Steps to complete	Dates	How I'm doing with this; what I need to adjust
Actively resist and protect against the exclusion of anyone		
Practice kindness and helpfulness		

REFLECTION:	
Did I reach my goal? If not, what kept me from reaching it?	
What was most satisfying?	
What worked well?	
What would I do differently next time?	
What more do I want to do or learn about this?	

3. Make sure that reflection (evaluation of the process and its outcomes) is part of the plan. This reflection can be done at the end of each step and at the end of the process; Figure 5.3 also includes reflection prompts.

Strategy 34: Boost Students' Control of Their Own Behavior

At school, being able regulate one's own behavior in appropriate ways is key to fitting into a peer group. Self-control is not always easy, but it results in satisfying connections and pride in oneself. It boosts autonomy and helps students accomplish their goals. Students who are able to regulate their behavior have improved interpersonal skills, higher self-esteem, better relationships, and increased happiness (de Ridder, Lensvelt-Mulders, Finkenauer, Stok, & Baumeister, 2012; Tangney, Baumeister, & Boone, 2004). All students should be able to exercise self-control, for their own well-being—and because it also contributes to a positive learning climate. For more on the benefits of self-control, see Strategy 23 (p. 73).

A sense of belonging affects the ability to develop self-control; when students' needs for belonging are met, their self-regulation abilities increase (Blackhart, Nelson, Winter, & Rockney, 2011; Strudwicke, 2000). The desire to belong, too, is a strong motivator to work at self-control (Baumeister & Leary, 1995).

When students recognize and name their feelings and have legitimate ways to express them (see the discussion of restorative practices in Strategy 22, p. 66), they feel better about themselves. As teachers and administrators, we have seen this in action: as self-control rises, students feel more powerful, autonomous, and proud of themselves. One of the best things that teachers can do is to intentionally teach the skills of self-management and give students tools for practicing these skills. Give them daily chances and supports for self-control. Help them believe that they *can* make good choices about and take responsibility for their own lives and behaviors. The following are two tools that we have used to spur student reflection and work on managing behavior.

A Reflective Plan for Behavior

Some teachers find behavior contracts to be great tools for self-management and improvement. Others find they don't work well—especially when they are just another version of the teacher controlling the behavior. And that's the problem: Often the contract is between *the student and the teacher* and so, in the end, the teacher is responsible for enforcing it.

We suggest thinking beyond the model in which a contract is used solely as a response to misbehavior—that is, of simply identifying a behavior and making an agreement about what will be stopped or changed.

To begin, **use the behavior contract as a practice for all students.** Introduce the concept of personal behavior agreements outside a setting where someone has done something wrong. This can follow other lessons or discussions about self-concept or self-awareness and about responsibility for one's own behavior. Doing this with all students shows the contract concept in a positive light—as a normal part of self-growth. It also prevents singling out individual students as the ones who need or are forced to use behavior contracts.

Ask students to **identify a behavior or pattern** that they would like to work to change, avoid, develop, or replace with something better. Ideally, they should set a goal for a positive behavior that they haven't practiced much or at all (e.g., gratitude, empathy, giving positive attention). You can provide a checklist of examples or have students suggest ideas. To further destigmatize the process for your students, develop a behavior contract for yourself, too. Let students see you setting goals for something you want to do differently or begin anew.

You can adapt a behavior agreement template for your class (see Figure 5.4) or **develop these plans** through an activity such as students filling out a graphic organizer, writing a letter, answering a series of questions, or having a one-on-one conversation with you. Your behavior agreement/plan/contract/tool might take a variety of forms, but it should be designed to do the following:

FIGURE 5.4

Template for a Student Behavior Agreement

The Background	
1. My behavior goal This is a behavior I wish to change, begin, replace, or stop.	
2. Background on this behavior This is why I identified this behavior as something I want start, stop, or change.	
3. Behavior reflection This is why I engage in this behavior—how I feel when I do it or how I feel later. OR: This is why I wish to develop this behavior—what I hope or expect will happen and how I expect or hope to feel.	
4. Effect on others This is how my behavior affects others. OR: This is how my new behavior might affect others and how I hope others will respond.	

The Plan	
1. Steps to take This is exactly what I will do, in the order I'll do it.	
2. Progress indicators This is what I will look for as evidence that I am making progress toward my goal.	
3. Goal achievement This is what I will look for as evidence that I have achieved my goal and changed my behavior in a way that is more than temporary.	
4. Help and support There are the people who can help or support me as I work to keep this agreement.	
5. Timeline and monitoring Here are the target dates and the name of the person who will help monitor my progress.	

I agree to this plan.

Signature: _____ Date: _____

Witness (co-monitor):

- Ask the student to describe the behavior in words.
- Allow for the student to describe the thoughts, feelings, and reasons (if they can be identified) accompanying the behavior.
- Examine outcomes of the behavior (e.g., what resulted from the behavior, how they felt about themselves during and after).
- Include reflection on others (if the behavior affects others)—asking the student to perceive the responses, feelings, and actions of others (how the other person was affected).
- Include identification of specific actions for alternate behaviors in the future.
- Allow students to identify sources of help they may need in following through with the plan.
- Set a schedule and plan for monitoring the agreement and evaluating the outcomes.
- Include an adult as a co-monitor (someone to check in with the student on progress), although students are the main monitors; the chosen adult is an assistant/encourager.
- Clearly have the purpose of the student making the plan and following it.

Take time to **discuss the experience.** Students can share their choices and plans (if they wish) or talk about what they learned from doing the task.

Follow up on these plans. Check in with each student to see that the monitoring was done. Take the time to evaluate the results of the process for each individual. Give students an opportunity to review and discuss the whole experience and to revise the plan or start from scratch and make something new.

If you **make this an occasional event for all students,** when a particular issue or challenge arises, students will feel more comfortable using this method to examine their behavior and working to make a change.

A Little Extra Motivation

Although we want all students to be intrinsically motivated to control themselves and behave appropriately, sometimes they need a little extrinsic boost. Simply put, some students need this bridge to learn the benefits of self-control.

When Patti was a teacher, she had an extremely challenging student in her class. "Alex" was new to the school, legally blind, biracial in a predominantly white community, and taller and more physically developed than the other students. He spoke very loudly and confronted other students over minor issues. The rest of the students were leery of being Alex's friend because he looked different, he was frequently disruptive, and his physical actions were intimidating to them. They treated him with caution, which only alienated him further and increased the difficulty he had managing his temper and adhering to the classroom agreements.

Patti worked with Alex's mother and the school district psychologist to implement a variety of strategies to help Alex improve his ability to self-manage, but the effect was limited. Eventually, at his mother's request, they created a behavioral contract wherein, if he met a specific level of success for 30 consecutive days, he could open the stereo set of his dreams that his mother had purchased and put at the top of his closet. This was a powerful motivator. When Alex eventually succeeded in managing himself for the 30 consecutive days, Patti was happy about this success but worried what would happen next. Would he revert to his old behaviors? He didn't. Once he discovered he could reliably manage his own behavior, he began to do it more consistently and fit in better—without the promise of a reward. Alex made friends and truly became part of the class. A contract that began with an extrinsic reward helped shift his behaviors and allowed him to experience the intrinsic reward of belonging.

Of course, not everyone who would benefit from the nudge of extrinsic motivation will have a stereo to work toward. You may need to get creative in selecting "rewards"—anything from lunch on you to the option of embarking on an individual study of interest for class credit. This is another place where your knowledge of and relationships with students can pay off.

Strategy 35: Promote Decision Making

Helping students become good decision makers is a worthy goal. Making wise, safe decisions is important to success in academics, self-management, self-advocacy, and working well with others. Students who don't have the opportunity to learn and practice decision-making strategies as part of their education have been done a disservice. From getting up in the morning and picking out what to wear to determining where to sit at lunch, how long to put off homework, or whether or not to send that social media post, students are constantly making decisions that have an academic, social, and behavioral effect. And their decisions can have a positive or negative effect on classroom culture and management and school success for others.

In working with students, remember that they are making their decisions without the benefit of fully developed executive function skills; they don't always consider or understand the consequences of their decisions. For a good overview of executive functioning and a list of related skills, see Rick Wormeli's 2013 article "Looking at Executive Function."

In order for students to learn to make healthy, positive decisions that benefit them as an individual as well as support a healthy classroom climate, they need to practice making decisions as individuals, in pairs, in small groups, and in large groups. And we owe it to our students to teach them multiple strategies they can use.

Assess Students' Decision-Making Skills

As with academic skills, it helps to first do a formative assessment of your students' decision-making skills. One teacher we know uses this approach: First, put students into small groups (about four each). Give each group a task that they must complete; they also must decide how they will complete it. For example, give each group a different short play and have them figure out who would play which role and how they would stage it. Have each group present its plan to the class, sharing how they made the decisions necessary to complete the task.

You may find that your student groups each use a different approach to the decision:

- One group might draw a name out of a hat for each character, task, or role.
- One group might discuss what they need to do and who wants to do what and work it out through conversation.
- One group might identify each student's strengths and make their choices based on the skills of the individuals.

It's also highly likely that in one or more groups, a student will just take over as leader and make all the decisions.

Here are some ways to introduce discussion topics and guide students in a self-assessment of their decision-making skills:

- Why do you think different strategies were used?
- Is any strategy better than another one?

- Are there other strategies that a group could have used?
- If you were to do this again, what strategy would you want to use?
- How can strategies help us make good decisions?
- How can you use strategies to help you determine how to complete school assignments, make decisions on your actions when you're angry, etc.?

Teach Decision-Making Strategies

Many students don't have go-to strategies for making decisions. Teaching these will help your students integrate effective decision making into their lives. When teaching these strategies, be sure to hold a discussion on what types of decisions the particular strategy will best support. Here are two you might try.

STP: Situation–Target–Plan. This is a good option for students to have when they need to slow down and think through a complicated course of action.

1. Identify the situation: *John and I don't get along. This project is due in three weeks, and I'm a procrastinator.*
2. Identify the target that you want to have happen: *For John and me to work together in class without arguing. I also want to complete my project two days before it's due so that I can be sure to turn it in on time.*
3. Determine your plan or strategy to meet your target: *John and I will meet with the counselor to talk out our problems and come to an agreement on how to get along better. I will ask my parents to help me create a calendar with due dates for when sections need to be completed. They will help monitor my progress.*

"The Ben Franklin Close." A middle-school principal we know had spent time as a real estate agent, so when it came time to make a decision, he would call upon this classic sales tactic (also known as "The Balance Sheet Close"). He'd draw a line down the middle of the page, put a plus at the top of one side and a minus on the other side, and proceed to list as many pros and cons as he could for a specific course of action.

Teaching your students to weigh the pros and the cons as a decision-making strategy is a good beginning. This strategy can be especially helpful for students who tend to make quick decisions that lead to unforeseen consequences for their actions or behavior (think social media).

Providing a go-to model and plenty of practice. Another way to teach students to make decisions more confidently is to give them regular opportunities to practice. Figure 5.5 provides a suggested flow chart of the process that you can present to your class and adapt to their activity. Start with simpler decisions—perhaps asking them to decide how to form groups in class, where to hold prom, or whether or not to post something on social media. Build to more complex decision making—which classes to take next year, what to do after high school, how to manage time commitments.

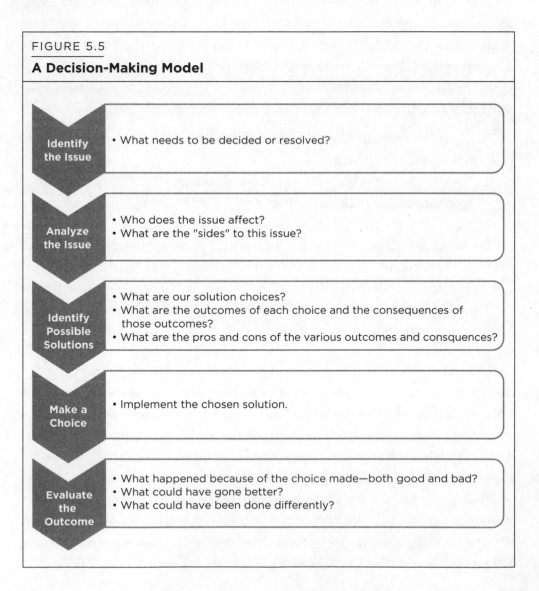

FIGURE 5.5

A Decision-Making Model

Identify the Issue
- What needs to be decided or resolved?

Analyze the Issue
- Who does the issue affect?
- What are the "sides" to this issue?

Identify Possible Solutions
- What are our solution choices?
- What are the outcomes of each choice and the consequences of those outcomes?
- What are the pros and cons of the various outcomes and consquences?

Make a Choice
- Implement the chosen solution.

Evaluate the Outcome
- What happened because of the choice made—both good and bad?
- What could have gone better?
- What could have been done differently?

Strategy 36: Value Different Perspectives

It can be challenging to understand and value the perspectives of others. Helping students see how others view and feel about things is important both for their academic knowledge and for their social-emotional growth and relationships with others. Perspective taking supports positive social relationships and generates feelings of closeness (Erie & Topolinski, 2017). When people develop perspective-taking skills, they are more likely to develop positive connections with people of different beliefs and less likely to stereotype others (Galinsky & Moskowitz, 2000; Gehlbach et al., 2015). Such skills are powerful tools to help students understand and accept one another's differences.

One of the best ways to help students begin to hear and value different perspectives is to have them actively take another's perspective—doing something as someone else. No person can precisely "walk in another's shoes." But staying in our own shoes, we can learn to see the world through the lens with which another experiences and makes sense of their world.

Perspectives Role-Play

Provide some scenarios that students can role-play—something out of your students' realm of experience. These could be made-up situations or situations students submit in writing (anonymously) that they have been in. With some creative thinking, sample scenarios can be related to content areas. Look for issues, ideas, or topics in social studies, science and technology, music choices, math processes, PE activities, or works and forms of art.

Perspectives of Life Experiences

This is a good activity for early in the year. Similar to Strategy 12's student-to-student introductions (see p. 38), this pairs exercise delves a little deeper and asks students to focus on active listening strategies.

Student A shares one to three important experiences from her life (e.g., moving from one place to another, gaining or losing a pet, birth of a sister or brother, death in the family, her best birthday present ever). Student B is to listen and ask questions to help understand the experience and its effect or influence. Then, the pairs reverse roles, with Student B sharing experiences and Student A being the listener. Come back together as a class and ask students to introduce their partners by retelling one of the stories; the retelling might need to happen over several days.

Perspectives Dance Cards

This is an effective activity for encouraging students to listen to one another's viewpoints and giving them practice "arguing" a perspective they may or may not agree with.

Step 1. Identify a particular topic or question for which there can be different viewpoints or answers. Divide the class into four groups, asking each group to take a different perspective on the topic or question. (For example, Patti remembers a time when her students were to pretend they were addressing the county commission regarding a land use issue that was forthcoming; the four groups she assigned were loggers, conservationists, homeowners, and forest service employees.) The members of the group do not actually have to hold the viewpoint they're assigned, although the group should agree on how to state their chosen perspective and its rationale.

Step 2. Give each student three "dance cards." Play music; when the music stops, each student is to have located another student from a group with a different perspective.

Step 3. In these pairs of students, one provides the perspective of the home group and its rationale; the other student briefly repeats or summarizes that position. When Student A agrees that the perspective has been heard accurately, the "dance card" is signed and the roles reverse.

Step 4. Play the music again and continue the process until each student has heard three other perspectives.

Step 5. Find a way (e.g., write a paragraph, hold a small-group discussion, discuss as a class) to have students synthesize the content and ideas they've learned and apply them to the lesson or classroom issue.

Make it a regular practice in your classroom to notice and explore others' perspectives. In his article, "Learning to Walk in Another's Shoes," Hunter Gehlbach (2017) suggested that teachers set these goals when teaching perspective taking:

- Regularly ask for multiple perspectives in classroom work and discussions.
- Teach students to withhold judgment while they seek to learn about the reasons behind the opinions or behaviors of others.

- Give students chances to predict what they think they've "read" or heard of another's perspectives.
- Give students chances to give feedback about whether others were correct or incorrect about what they've "read." (pp. 11–12)

When students' perspectives are heard and valued, they are much more likely to feel as though they belong and matter. This is true for both the students sharing perspectives and for the students who are listening or watching—and thus learning about others. Those who feel that their classmates and teachers are actually interested in "reading" them and understanding them are much more likely to contribute to a positive school and classroom climate.

Strategy 37: Practice Conflict Resolution

We all have family members, friends, and colleagues who would do just about anything to avoid dealing with conflict. But let's face it: conflict is a part of life, and teachers must help students understand this. Depending on how one chooses to deal with it, either conflict can be a positive part of life and an opportunity for growth, or it can develop into a situation that breaks up friendships, causes hard feelings, or even results in physical harm.

When students develop skills in conflict resolution, they gain an ability that will serve them well throughout their lives. Increased success with conflict resolution helps students become more independent, self-assured, and mature. It improves peer relationships and raises feelings of safety and belonging. And a great side effect of good conflict resolution practices is this: many classroom management issues are prevented or defused—leaving more time for quality instruction.

Class Discussion and Role-Play

The concept of an escalator is an apt analogy for handling conflicts. Ask students to think about conflicts this way: During a conflict, the words and actions of the persons involved can take them "up" the escalator, with the conflict escalating (greater and greater distress). Or their words and actions can take them "down" the escalator, with the conflict de-escalating and being resolved (less distress and more relief).

Continue a discussion of conflicts by considering the following questions (in pairs, small groups, or as a whole group):

- What examples have you seen of a conflict escalating or de-escalating?
- What words and actions can take you "up" the escalator?
- What words and actions can take you "down" the escalator?
- What feelings come up the most often during conflicts?
- How do your feelings affect the way you deal with conflict?
- What kinds of outcomes can result when there is a conflict (i.e., win-win; win-lose, lose-lose)?

As an activity, break students into groups, ask them to identify a common conflict, and then arrange a role-play or a few role-play scenarios with various outcomes to the conflict.

A Classroom Protocol for Resolving Conflict

There are many models of conflict resolution available. If your school or team has adopted a particular model, then use it. If not, you might have your students create a simple five- to six-step model that can be used in your classroom. We present here one way to break down the steps of a conflict-resolution process that you can teach students and practice in the classroom. You might also develop these steps as a class, with students' input.

1. **Cool off.** Take a deep breath.
2. **Define the conflict.** Be specific in describing the problem. What is the specific issue, and how did it come about? The more information you have about the cause of the problem, the easier it is to arrive at a good solution. The focus is on keeping the relationship.
3. **Find a common goal,** something to agree on. Don't make assumptions, and try to understand one another's point of view. (Remind students of the active listening strategies covered in Strategy 32.) Is there more happening here than the problem of the moment? Are there underlying issues one student can see that another might not?
4. **Agree on the best way to resolve the conflict,** and create a plan to meet the common goal. This includes identifying any barriers that could keep you from meeting your goal.
5. **Acknowledge the solution,** and decide what responsibilities each person has in the resolution.

Cease and Desist Requests

There are times when a pattern of conflict develops in which one student is persistently harassed by another. In these cases, action must be taken for an immediate cessation of the behavior. In addition, the students may need a "time-out" from one another.

Here's an approach we've used that helps stop the offensive action, empowers the person being harassed, and leads to some restorative practices for the harasser.

Step 1: Introduce students to the concept of a cease and desist order. This is a legal measure and a serious one. It requires certain practices to stop and is often issued by a judge. For students, frame the idea of a process that could lead to immediate relief from the situation for the harassed and the possibility of a change in the behavior.

Step 2: Clarify the concept of harassment for students. *Harassment* is an action or combination of actions causing someone to feel threatened, belittled, discriminated against, afraid, angry, hurt, ashamed, or embarrassed. Harassment is defined by the one being harassed, not the harasser; it is the harassed person's experience that matters. Explicitly state that any harassment must stop; the harasser must "cease and desist."

As part of a class discussion, ask students to identify every form of harassment they know that could happen or has happened in schools. It may be wide-ranging and include such things as verbal and physical aggression; emotional harassment; intimidation; and racial, ethnic, religious, sexual, or gender harassment. It can take the form of notes, letters, emails, texts, or social media posts. With students, identify specific actions within these categories. You may need to emphasize that harassment can include things that students might think of as just joking around (e.g., making noises at someone, muttering threats, teasing, tripping, staring, or pointing).

Step 3: Incorporate class input into a Cease and Desist Form and process students can use when necessary. The form lists the actions the class has identified as harassing. A student who feels harassed fills out the form, checking off the items on the list that apply. The teacher reviews the "complaint" and, if it is justified, brings the students involved together to discuss the problem.

Follow the restorative justice process of talking *with* students, not *at* them (see Strategy 22 in Chapter 3). The student being harassed should feel safe to share feelings generated by the harassment. Your role is also to help the harasser to examine the motivation and feelings behind and during the behavior, and how it has affected both students. The goal is for the harasser to come to a place where the harassment will stop permanently.

Step 4: Ask the student involved in doing the harassment to sign the Cease and Desist Form. This is an acknowledgment that the behavior will cease and that further harassment could result in additional consequences. If you have done your work with the class, students know that further steps will have to be taken if the harassment does not stop or if it changes form to a different kind of harassment.

Step 5: Ask the students involved to have no further contact with each other, including staring at or talking with each other. If they are in a classroom or classes together, have the students sit a distance from each other so as to minimize contact. If they share the same lunch period, they should sit at different tables and not participate in the same activity at the same time.

How well does this work? The time apart is critical for both parties. Sometimes further consequences will be needed, but usually there is a solution agreeable to the harassed student and constructive for the harasser. Most often (about 90 percent of the time, actually), the students involved will show up, say they want to be friends again, and ask if you will tear up the document.

6

Belonging Thrives on Engaging, Student-Centered Instruction

When I don't get what the teacher is teaching, I don't feel connected to my class or the teacher.
a 6th grader

This chapter addresses quality instructional practices that deepen belonging while promoting effective classroom management. The strategies here focus on such elements of effective teaching as giving students choice and involvement in their learning, active learning and effective questioning techniques, giving clear directions, planning for smooth transitions, getting and giving effective feedback, and student self-assessment.

Effective classroom management depends on effective instruction. Lessons that are engaging, student-centered, well organized, and delivered with appropriate pacing and transitions positively affect student behavior and promote belonging. Conversely, when lesson goals and delivery are hazy or disorganized, when students are not actively involved or see little relevance of activities, when little choice or personal investment is offered to students, when some students are not "getting it," or when you as a teacher are just "winging it" without plans, classroom management can go downhill quickly—along with students' sense of belonging and their resulting learning. When students experience the joys of personal academic challenge and accomplishment, their sense of belonging rises and they behave better.

In 2004, a group of educators, along with representatives of health and government sectors, got together in a conference dedicated to synthesizing a set of core principles for school connectedness. This work involved closely reviewing the current research and sharing information gathered from across the represented sectors. Among the critical requirements for school belonging published in their final document were these: "High academic expectations and rigor coupled with support for learning" and "Hiring and supporting capable teachers skilled in content, teaching techniques, and classroom management to meet each learner's needs" (Wingspread, 2004). Academic success (including students' beliefs that they can succeed), feelings of connectedness to school, and student behavior have powerful reciprocal relationships (Akey, 2006; Anderman, 2003; Goodenow, 1993a, 1993b; Roeser, Midgley, & Urdan, 1996).

A 2009 U.S. Centers for Disease Control report on school connectedness names "effective teaching methods to foster a positive learning environment" (p. 13) as one of its key strategies to promote increased connectedness. *Effective teaching* includes such practices as interactive and experiential activities to engage students in learning and personalize information; flexible instructional strategies that allow for teachable moments and personalization in academic lessons; teaching methods that are conducive to diverse needs and learning styles; group projects; and teaching problem-solving skills, critical thinking, questioning, and reflection. Additional practices that are critical to academic success and accompanying positive behavior are clear expectations, teachers helping students reach goals, support for student self-efficacy, tasks that are perceived as interesting and important, and focus on individual mastery (Ames, 1992; Eccles & Wigfield, 1995; Roeser et al., 1996).

Strategy 38: Set the Instructional Tone for Belonging

The first day of school is prime real estate for setting both the behavioral and instructional tone for the year. In earlier chapters, we described strategies for establishing a positive behavioral tone. Here we share an effective strategy for sending students the messages that the classroom is about learning, and that learning will be exciting and fun.

In her first few years as a middle school principal, Laurie had a brilliant idea (or so she thought): Teachers would divide the student handbook into seven sections, and then, on the first day of school, they would read and review with students a single section during each period. In 1st period, every teacher would cover Section 1; in 2nd period, Section 2; and so on. By the end the day, every student would understand the handbook and be prepared to follow the rules as written. As you might guess, that didn't work very well. Teachers used various (often half-hearted) approaches to satisfy the principal's "request," but none of the tactics had much of an effect on student behavior. Laurie did learn an important lesson: students don't behave and make good decisions because a handbook tells them to do so.

Laurie also learned that she was a big part of why the first day of school was anything but exciting for the students. She was so concerned about students following the rules and teachers establishing clear guidelines that she lost sight of what she really wanted: teachers being passionate about teaching and students being enthusiastic about learning. Spending the first day, and sometimes the first *week,* on rules wasn't contributing to either of these aims. Instead, it was contributing to disconnection. Students didn't bond with one another. They had no chance to experience the satisfaction of being together, working together, or belonging to a group. And they certainly weren't learning anything of real significance—and that included the rules.

The "A-Day" Mindset

Having learned that lesson, Laurie gathered the school staff together, and they decided on a new approach. From then on, the first day of school was called "A-Day," which meant bringing your best—your "A" game. It meant engaging students in a lesson they wouldn't forget. It meant transmitting messages and starting other processes that let students know that engagement, participation, learning something new, relationships, connection (aka belonging), and fun were of prime importance.

Whatever else happens on A-Day, students leave having experienced great instruction and the joy of doing or finding out something new. They are so busy learning, cooperating, and enjoying themselves as members of the group that the patterns for meaningful class involvement are well under way from the beginning of the school year.

Take, for example, a middle-grades science lesson on dissecting rats (just the right hook for a group of young adolescents). The teacher prepares well ahead of time, posts lab rules on the wall, and has science goggles and instruments ready to go. After a review of safety guidelines and an explanation of the activity, students work in pairs collaboratively to dissect rats—on the first day of school! They keep records of their "finds" and discuss and share their results *together*. One thing is certain: The students will follow every direction as requested and go home with something really cool to share. This "something cool," by the way, doesn't involve asking parents to sign a six-page syllabus or behavior code—that can be saved for later.

This type of class experience shows students that this class will be about engagement and learning. The teacher's primary focus isn't on looking for and expecting misbehavior at every turn. Instead, with a fun, engaging, and effective A-Day lesson plan, teachers

- Demonstrate effective, relevant instructional practices;
- Show students that they can be successful working together;
- Establish the value of active learning;
- Place a high value on learning and on application of knowledge;
- Set a process that enables every student to succeed;
- Assure students that this class will be a safe and fun place to learn; and
- Maintain strong classroom management.

The "B-Day" Mindset

Before long, the staff realized that A-Day is also "B-Day"—a *belonging day*. Not only does it set the instructional tone you want, but this memorable learning experience of group involvement and satisfying success also clearly sends a message that the classroom is a place where everyone belongs. Student belonging is bolstered by the experience of accomplishing something together with others, of being a necessary part of making something exciting happen, of personally meeting an academic requirement, of feeling competent, and of laughing with others. Wouldn't it be great if every day were an A-Day and a B-Day for all students?

Beyond the First Day

Maybe you can't dissect rats or shoot off rockets every day, but powerful, engaging, and relevant instruction can be the norm beyond Day 1. The first days set a pattern that needs to deepen and broaden. Remember: engaged, productive students who are learning new things and having personal academic success are less likely to be disruptive or uncooperative. They are also more likely to feel like satisfied members of a unified group.

Identify the components of your instructional approach. Make a checklist of the kinds of learning experiences and outcomes that are goals for *all* your instruction—all year. Be sure to stretch yourself and add to the list some you haven't used or that you rarely use. Use it to guide your instructional plans. Your list should include some or all of these:

- **Scaffolded success:** Clear expectations for assignments, support for struggling students, experiences of mastery, differentiation
- **Varying assignment formats:** Cooperative work; inquiry, analysis, evaluation experiences; independent projects and lessons
- **Varying content delivery:** Explanations or lectures, demonstrations, discussions, learning centers, peer teaching, literature circles, technology
- **Motivating experiences:** Active learning, student choice, discussion and constructive debate, cross-disciplinary studies, creating
- **Important learning skills:** Thoughtful questioning techniques, problem solving, decision making, higher-order thinking skills
- **Relevant content:** Personalized, culturally affirming learning opportunities; engaging topics and activities that students identify as relevant to their lives; "real-world" problems and issues that empower students to have influence in their communities
- **Ownership of learning:** Reflection on progress, feedback, responsibility for own work, goal setting, and progress monitoring

And don't forget to include fun and laughter.

Strategy 39: Practice Dynamic Instruction

Intentionally planning for engaging, dynamic instruction is perhaps the most critical aspect of successful classroom management and has the added benefit of creating a class where students feel like they are where they want to be.

Plan Ahead

Dynamic instruction takes forethought. Creating a well-organized plan to implement in an intentional manner will go a long way toward effective classroom management. Engaging lesson plans include time for discussion and reflection by students. If you want your students to learn the material, it's important for them to have opportunities to discuss the content with the class, with a partner, in small groups, and with you.

Think through all the details and steps of a lesson, especially if there's an area where you think you might have difficulties, because it's harder to think on your feet if things go wrong. Teachers who are confident in their subject matter inspire confidence and respect from students and greatly minimize discipline problems. On the other hand, for a teacher who can plan and implement a fairly well-designed lesson plan but struggles to recalibrate and explain content in another way if students don't understand, things can go downhill rather quickly. And if your lesson includes the use of technology, always have a backup plan in mind in case the technology doesn't work the way you'd planned.

Having an organizational structure in mind will help your lesson flow smoothly. Here is one option:

1. **Identify your standard or objective.** Decide what it is you want the students to know or be able to do. Share your standard or objective in "kid-friendly" language. Tell them what they will be learning and why it's important, useful, and relevant in their present and future.

2. **Develop a question that answers the standard or objective.** The question should encourage and guide exploration of the topic and point students toward the desired knowledge and skills.

3. **Conduct a warm-up, where students review and assess.** This helps focus students on content right from the start.

4. **Use an activating strategy to hook and motivate students.** Decide on your opening, an anticipatory set that connects the new learning to past learning, narrows the focus, and involves everyone.

5. **Conduct a minilesson to provide information, elicit information, question, model a process, or facilitate groups.** Use the gradual release of responsibility model (see pp. 86–87), where you explain or demonstrate the skill or process ("I do it alone"), work through the skill or process with students ("We do it together"), give students a chance to practice with others ("You do it together"), and then finally release students to work independently ("You do it alone").

6. **Have students read, listen, discuss, research, or work in groups.** Check for understanding: How will you know students are ready to "move

on"? Will you question a sampling of students, ask for a thumbs-up or group choral response, or use student self-assessment or a teacher-made assessment? How will students practice? Will practice be guided (with a teacher monitoring), conducted in a group activity or stations, or done independently? Will there be homework?

7. **Give students an opportunity to summarize what they have learned.** Have students answer the essential question of the lesson or review important concepts and vocabulary.

There are many lesson plan models available, and some schools have a required format. The important thing to remember is to *use the steps of a lesson plan as a decision-making model, not as a checklist.* You do not have to do every step in every lesson, but you should think through the steps and have a good reason for doing (or not doing) them.

Check Your Materials and Your Language

Nothing can derail a lesson faster than being unprepared and unorganized. Make sure that your materials are ready to use and that you have a plan for distributing them to your students. Cleanup is equally important, so develop a routine for how things get cleaned up and put away at the end of the class or the day. Messy classrooms can sometimes give the impression that the teacher might be lax in other areas, including dealing with behavioral issues.

Part of your well-stocked toolkit includes the language you will use to prompt student participation and response. A question that starts with "Can anyone tell me . . ." or "Does anyone know . . ." is likely to be met with blank stares. Are you sending the message that you don't really believe everyone can answer your question? Compare that type of question to "Think about the challenge the main character was facing. Do you think she handed it correctly? Everyone be ready to give your answer when I call on you." Give some wait time before you start calling on students. Sending the message that you expect everyone to participate encourages active participation.

Monitor Students . . . and Keep Monitoring Them

With practice, your "teacher sensors" can be finely tuned to your students' emotional state and sense of belonging such that you can monitor the classroom for potential problems while you are teaching. Walk around the room; simply moving to an area where the disruptions might occur can prevent them. Change your pattern of moving around the room, and vary your routine. It's important to face your students, but if they can't anticipate where you'll be teaching from, it can help minimize management issues.

As tempting as it is to try to grade a few tests or complete paperwork at your desk when students are involved in group or individual seatwork, don't fall into the trap of doing so. If you're involved in something at your desk and students don't think you're watching, they have more opportunities to misbehave. Disengaging from your class also means you're less likely to notice when students are struggling—with either academics or behavior.

Vary Your Instructional Practices

There are many methods of instruction and instructional strategies and practices; it's easy to settle into two or three with which you are really comfortable. Although there's nothing wrong with using your strengths, it helps to occasionally examine your instructional practices. Consider which ones you use and how often, and if there are others you can implement both to improve student engagement and achievement and to minimize classroom disruptions.

There's a wealth of resources from colleagues, books, and the internet about effective teaching practices, and we encourage you to seek these out, expand your repertoire, and refine your practice. To start, you might want to review the following list of instructional strategies and make note of any that you are unfamiliar with or feel less than confident using. Which of these are you using now? Are there some you might be *over*using?

- Explanations and lectures
- Demonstrations
- Discussions
- Cooperative pairs and groups
- Investigations or inquiries
- Experiments
- Research
- Cooperative learning groups
- Learning centers
- Peer teaching
- Active learning (with movement)
- Discovery

- Differentiation
- Socratic circles
- Creating
- HOTS (higher-order thinking skills)
- Team teaching and co-teaching
- Literature circles
- Cross-disciplinary integration work
- Individual work
- Independent studies
- Technology (in the hands of students)
- Reflections (on academic work and behavior)

Varying your approaches expands your reach and gives you more data on what works best with your students.

Strategy 40: Teach Students to Assess Their Own Learning

Self-assessment—a dynamic process in which students self-monitor, self-evaluate, and identify correctives to learn—is a critical skill that enhances student motivation and achievement (McMillan & Hearn, 2008). When learners assess their own performance, they develop important metacognitive skills and make academic gains. The process also boosts awareness of their own learning behaviors, strengths, and needs and leads to increases in self-efficacy, critical thinking skills, responsibility for their own learning and self-management, and academic independence (Bandura, 1997; Rolheiser & Ross, 2001; Zimmerman & Schunk, 2011).

Academic self-assessment is a valuable component of assessment in any classroom. It boosts learning and metacognition when used as a way to gauge understanding and progress rather than just a way to check for success or failure at meeting a goal. Self-assessment is most valuable when the assessment is "grounded in explicit, relevant, evaluative criteria followed by an opportunity to relearn and/or revise" (Andrade, 2019, para. 11). When students self-assess in this way, they

> learn to chart a learning path informed by their specific funds of knowledge [knowledge and skills of their daily routines], identify areas of challenge, add strategies to their unique learning repertoire, and even learn to ask for what they need in the classroom. That's empowerment, just one of the many benefits of FA [formative assessment] . . . , [a] key to creating the foundation for a classroom culture of learning. (McCoy, 2020, para. 12)

Self-reflection can highlight for students how they approach their learning—teaching them to recognize and analyze their academic processes, strengths, styles, and needs for improvement. When students reflect, they get a picture of their attitudes toward learning and how those may affect what they do. When the reflection is specific to a project (during or after completion), it gets at how things went and worked on that particular task. Self-reflection skills also help students set future goals for the way they will tackle academic tasks.

With *self-evaluation*, students assess their performance against some standard in order to judge the quality of their work. The criteria are often established in a rubric, scoring guide, checklist, or table of project requirements and goals. Regardless of what standards are being used, it's critical that students understand the academic guidelines with which they will evaluate themselves—and even better if they participate in forming these.

If students are to develop the skills of academic self-assessment, they need to be taught how to evaluate their processes and outcomes and how to reflect on the experience.

Practicing Self-Assessment in the Classroom

Here are some useful tips to help ensure effective student self-assessment.

Know what student self-assessment involves. Too often, activities in which students evaluate their work are merely a checkup on a grade—intended to gauge the level to which they succeeded on a specific task or mastered a specific concept. Self-assessments requiring scoring with a final rating of excellent, good, fair, or weak, or percentage complete/correct, are not enough. This type of activity is summative assessment alone and does not produce the full benefits of self-assessment. Reflection *and* evaluation against a standard need to be combined. There must be a learning-oriented purpose to self-assessment—not just learning a particular concept but also learning about how one learned (Andrade, 2019).

Be a role model of self-reflection. Think of the times you have taught a lesson that didn't go well and asked yourself, "Where did it go wrong?" On the other hand, you might have taught an engaging lesson to a class of engaged learners and wonder, "How did that happen?" Whenever you think through what transpired in the classroom, you are practicing self-reflection. Successful teachers do this all the time, almost automatically, with the goal of improving the way they teach and the ways students learn. The process helps you gain insight into your strengths and areas for growth; it can also reinforce your instructional practices. It's a practice to intentionally continue and expand.

Share your reflections with students so they can see how the evaluation process works. You can take this process to the next level by sharing your insights with your students. Don't be afraid to admit errors and course-correct: "I reflected on our science lesson yesterday and realized you were confused because I didn't give very clear directions. I'm sorry that happened. Here's what I should have said...." Don't be afraid to ask for advice: "Do you have any suggestions about how I can give clearer directions?" After a lesson that went particularly well, you might stop and say, "That was really fun! Here's what I think I did to get you interested and involved with the material.... Do you think that's what did the trick?" Whenever you share your own thinking processes with students, you help them to become more metacognitive about their learning and actions.

Follow consistent processes for self-evaluation. According to researchers Carol Rolheiser and John Ross (2001), teachers and students should follow these steps in the evaluation part of assessment:

1. **Define the criteria for a particular assignment.** Involve students in this task, so that the criteria for evaluation will be a combination of teacher-specified goals and individual student goals. Take time to hash out and clarify the criteria with students.

2. **Apply the criteria.** Students use the criteria to evaluate their own work. When students are new at this, model the process and give examples.

3. **Give feedback on student self-evaluations.** Find ways to incorporate peer and teacher feedback on individual self-evaluation. The goal here is to help students get better at applying criteria.

4. **Develop plans to set new goals**. Provide support for students as they decide whether they achieved goals, how well they achieved goals, and what they can do to produce better-quality work in the future.

One caution: don't overwhelm your students with a self-reflection after every assignment; save it for the important ones—those that engage them with big ideas, key concepts, essential skills—so it doesn't become just another hoop to jump through.

Reflect with a Selfie

To ease students into the practice of self-reflection, ask them to take a selfie—of themselves as learners. You might offer them choices, too, allowing them to write a letter, make a diagram, create a poster, show a series of photos, or record a video monologue. To keep the spirit of the "selfie," you might want to require that one aspect of their product be visual. Create a list of items they can include, from which they should choose three to five to incorporate, such as the following:

- I learn best by . . .
- I begin and complete assignments by . . .
- The best conditions for me to learn are . . .
- My strongest academic abilities are . . .
- The best kinds of learning tasks are . . .
- My system of organization is . . .
- I have a hard time with . . .
- The most exciting part of doing an assignment is . . .
- The hardest part of doing an assignment is . . .
- I wish I could do better or differently as a student with . . .

You might also invite students to add items to the list.

Reflect with a Form

Self-assessment forms or graphics can help students learn and practice these skills. A form can focus on academic reflection, evaluation, or both aspects of self-assessment.

Evaluation templates need to be fairly task-specific. A writing rubric displays objectives for a written essay, narrative, or argument, along with scores for and descriptions of different levels of quality. A math rubric outlines the components of a problem-solving process and provides descriptive criteria and scores for various levels of performance. A PE task is evaluated with a checklist defining numbers of a particular exercise or times for completing physical tasks.

A form for self-reflection, however, can be more generalized. Figure 6.1 provides an example that can apply to a variety of assignments or tasks and be adapted to your grade level or class. Such a form could serve as a guide for a teacher–student interview or peer–peer discussion, rather than a written response. Whatever forms you use, definitely give students the task of designing

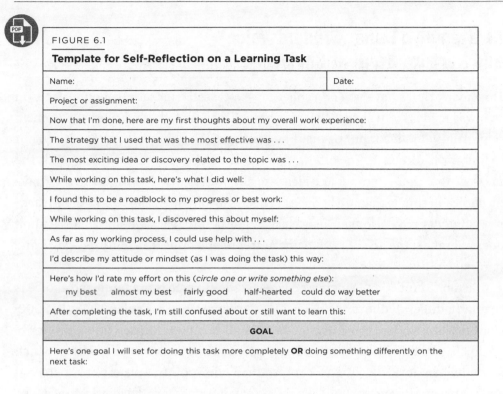

FIGURE 6.1

Template for Self-Reflection on a Learning Task

Name:	Date:

Project or assignment:
Now that I'm done, here are my first thoughts about my overall work experience:
The strategy that I used that was the most effective was . . .
The most exciting idea or discovery related to the topic was . . .
While working on this task, here's what I did well:
I found this to be a roadblock to my progress or best work:
While working on this task, I discovered this about myself:
As far as my working process, I could use help with . . .
I'd describe my attitude or mindset (as I was doing the task) this way:
Here's how I'd rate my effort on this (*circle one or write something else*):   my best   almost my best   fairly good   half-hearted   could do way better
After completing the task, I'm still confused about or still want to learn this:
GOAL
Here's one goal I will set for doing this task more completely **OR** doing something differently on the next task:

or contributing to their creation. And don't miss the opportunity to use this reflection form and process yourself. You, too, can set learning tasks. Let students see you evaluating your own accomplishments and progress.

Other Ways to Reflect

Teaching the process of self-reflection is limited only by your creativity. Here are some other ways students can reflect on completed work or a project:

- Respond to specific questions in writing. ("What do you like about this piece of work?" "What grade would you give yourself and why?" "What do you still not understand?" "What might you do differently the next time?")
- Draw a picture or diagram of the steps you used to complete this project.
- Write a letter to the teacher explaining what you did to complete the project.
- Write a letter to yourself explaining what you discovered about how you learn best.
- Make a graph of effort, satisfaction, interest, and value.
- Write journal or learning log entries.

Strategy 41: Honor Student Voice and Nurture Student Choice

How many times have you or a colleague expressed frustration about a decision that was made "from above" that affects your teaching—but you weren't given an opportunity to give input or make suggestions? You simply have no choice but to follow the directive. Too often, students can feel the same way. This sends the message that their opinions and ideas are not wanted or valued and that they have no choice in things that are happening in classroom operations or in their learning. Students may also feel their voice is not being heard when the curriculum does not reflect the diversity of their classroom or it appears to only recognize one particular point of view.

School connection is increased when student voice is nurtured and choice is regularly integrated into their school experience (Assor, Kaplan, & Roth, 2002; Cook-Sather, 2006; Deci & Ryan, 1987; Fielding, 2004; Flutter, 2007; Flutter & Ruddick, 2004; Katz & Assor, 2007). *Student voice* refers to the extent to which students are able and free to express their viewpoints, suggestions, personal experiences, and backgrounds. The topic of voice goes beyond expression; it also includes the degree to which student's expressions are invited, listened to, valued, seriously considered, and acted upon. It includes the level of their involvement and investment in school life. *Student choice* refers to offering students options in classroom practices, including their own learning experiences. These are not just selections from a list of options; they are choices that involve a student's action and participation and support development of the student's competence and autonomy.

In this strategy, we focus on both student voice and choice in their own learning because they are integrally related in the classroom learning setting. In the context of academic activities, this means asking students for their input, opinions, experiences, evaluations, and feedback on the things they are learning. It means providing students with meaningful choices in matters of academic work, particularly their own individual learning tasks. Ask for student opinions and offer them choices about

- What they will learn,
- How they will learn,
- With whom they will learn,

- How their learning process will be monitored,
- Their learning timeline,
- Specific learning tasks,
- How they will communicate or share what they learn, and
- How their learning will be evaluated.

Assess Readiness

Assessing the level of your student's self-management skills can help you determine how much opportunity you can offer students for more authentic voice and choice in your course or classroom. Student voice and choice in an advanced senior English class will not look the same as that in a beginning freshman English class or in a 5th grade class. You might begin by offering students specific options from which they may choose; as they mature or gain practice with both voice and choice, give them more freedom in determining their learning opportunities.

Listen to Students' Voices

Students already have voices. It's the school's and teacher's job to honor student voice by inviting students to speak, listen, and learn. Here are a few ways to solicit, honor, and strengthen student input and opinions:

- Plan for student input, questions, and responses in every lesson.
- During learning activities, stop and ask questions ("What does this remind you of?" "How can you use this information in your life?").
- Make student presentations a regular part of instruction. Even better, give students opportunities to teach a concept, process, or skill that they have mastered.
- Ask students for "lesson dissections." Let them evaluate a lesson you've taught, telling what helped them learn, what they needed that was not in the lesson, the high points, the confusions, and the effective techniques.
- Follow Strategy 17's suggestion for students to take part in or take major responsibility in conferences with parents. Let them be "in charge" of sharing information about their learning, their work, their progress, their accomplishments, and areas of needed growth or improvement.
- Design and use a system of kind but honest and helpful feedback—for students to give to one another, to themselves, or to the teacher.

- Use reflections and surveys as ways to gather student observations, experiences, and suggestions. Even better, give students the task of designing the surveys.

Offer Students Choices

Offer opportunities for choice that are appropriate to students' age and abilities. Because many students have not had a lot of experience with choice, at first you may need to give limited and structured options. But as soon and often as possible, broaden the options, or, when appropriate, have "open" options so students can follow their own interests and questions. Think about giving choices in what students will do to learn or practice something and in how and when they will show what they've learned. Here are some choices students might make:

- As a team, decide which project out of five your group will complete.
- Choose a book from a list for a book-share activity. If there's a book you want to read that isn't on the list, write a note to the teacher about that choice.
- Choose from among several ways to share the results of a report or investigation you've done or a question you've researched. These can include oral, visual, written, electronic, artistic, and multimedia options. If you think of an option that has not been suggested, make a case for that to be the one you choose.
- Work by yourself on a particular task or work quietly with a partner.
- Working as a small group, choose one of the classroom procedures related to academic activities and write a brief evaluation of how that is currently operating or succeeding in the classroom.
- When it's time for individual presentations in class, choose your time slot on a schedule prepared by the teacher. Choose whether you'll present to the whole class or to a smaller group.
- Edit your own paper or choose to have a peer edit your work.
- From a list of tasks to be accomplished for an assignment, choose the order in which you'll do these. Identify an optional one to drop from the list.
- Choose from a list of options the way you want an assignment to be evaluated. Suggest another option if you have an idea that is not on the list.
- Write or diagram an original math or science problem to demonstrate that you understand the concept or operation.
- Choose a topic of your interest and expertise for a demonstration on how to do something.

Opportunities for student voice and choice enhance engagement, participation, autonomy, self-esteem, and responsibility—all crucial components of instruction. As well, regular student input and student choice are all factors that contribute to positive influences on classroom life and management.

For a more in-depth discussion of and more strategies for incorporating voice and choice, see our book, *Middle School: A Place to Belong and Become* (Barron & Kinney, 2018). The strategies there are useful or adaptable for many levels below and above the middle grades.

Strategy 42: Help Students Make Friends with Failure

Have you ever refused to try something new because you were afraid of failing or making a fool of yourself? Although the book *Failure Is Not an Option* (Blankstein, 2009) offers solid principles that help students succeed, we've never been a fan of the title. In reality, failure is *always* an option—the possibility of failure always accompanies the act of trying. Countless writers, celebrities, famous people, and "ordinary" people have told stories about how risk and failure are part of the fabric of their successful or satisfying lives. Ellen DeGeneres (2011) has observed that taking risks teaches two equally important lessons: sometimes you will succeed, and sometimes you will fail. Michael Jordan famously said, "I have missed more than 9,000 shots in my career. I've lost almost 300 games. Twenty-six times, I've been trusted to take the game winning shot and missed. I've failed over and over and over again in my life. And that is why I succeed" (Nike, 2012).

In today's world of high-stakes testing—exacerbated with a goodly amount of helicopter (hovering nearby) and lawn-mower (chopping down obstacles) parenting—students are often afraid of failure. In classrooms, much of challenging student behavior can be directly attributed to a series of failures that have led a student to give up, stop trying, and act out. Many students have experienced failure after failure, in both school and life, and no longer believe they are capable of learning or succeeding. What if teachers were able to help students embrace and learn from failure rather than become dejected and give up because of it?

Most educators we know are dedicated to helping students succeed. At the same time, educators are increasingly aware of the need to teach students how to handle disappointment, distress, and failure. Letting them fail and guiding them to learn from their mistakes is essential to building resilience and helping them become confident, successfully functioning adults.

According to Dr. Amanda Mintzer, a clinical psychologist at the Child Mind Institute,

> the ability to tolerate imperfection—that something is not going exactly your way—is oftentimes more important to learn than whatever the content subject is. Building that skill set is necessary for kids to be able to become more independent and succeed in future endeavors, whether it's personal goals, academic goals, or just learning how to effectively deal with other people. (quoted in Arky, n.d.)

It's your job to help students see that, though it may seem rather weird, failure is their friend. You can help them see that failure, combined with hard work and effort, leads to learning. How? Engage them in experiences that show them that they can get back up after being knocked down—by mistakes, disappointment, or poor choices. Instead of scrambling to shield them from failure, teach them to embrace it. In our many years of professional observations in our roles as educators, we've noticed that students who become comfortable with failing, learning from failure, and trying again also become more comfortable with themselves and more empathetic toward others. The gains they make from embracing failure translate into increased belonging and fewer classroom management issues. The following are some tips for addressing failure with your students.

Show Empathy

First of all, acknowledge the feelings of hurt, disappointment, frustration, and self-doubt. Say it out loud: "I can see that you are really disturbed by this. I know you hoped for a better result." Empathy will go further and be far more helpful than saying, "It will get better" or "Shake it off." Show students, by your response, that it's no big deal to mess up; they have permission to make mistakes.

Share Stories of Failure

Don't be afraid to share your own stories of failures. It's important that students see you as someone who perseveres and learns from your mistakes. It could be a humorous anecdote about a cooking failure or similar mishap, or something a little more painful: an election you lost when you were in school, a lesson that didn't go as planned, or poor decisions you made in the past. Students often think teachers don't make (or admit to making) mistakes. Let them know you are human; everyone makes mistakes. The important thing is to keep trying and learn from them.

YouTube is full of videos of celebrities and successful people relating their failures and how they handled the experience, some of which you might also share with your students. Just the other day we watched a video of Oprah Winfrey (2017) in which she spoke about getting demoted from a news anchor position and reassigned as an interviewer on a local talk show. What felt at first like a failure led to her discovering her true calling.

Invoke the Power of *Yet*

Yet is such a good word to add to your teaching vocabulary. "You're right; you don't understand how to do long division . . . *yet!* But we'll work on it together, and I'll help you get it." "We're going to be learning a new process to work with pottery; it'll be different, and you won't find it easy . . . *yet!* But we'll take it step by step, and I'll help you understand how to do it." "I'm sorry you haven't *yet* mastered the ability to stay in your seat when I'm teaching, but we're going to keep working on that." Using the word *yet* when students are struggling implies it's fine not to know something, but they eventually will learn how to do it.

Teach the Concept of Mindsets

Helping students understand the basics of Carol Dweck's mindset research will also help them learn to deal with failures and understand the importance of effort and perseverance over just being "smart." Those with a *fixed* mindset (i.e., ability and talents are finite and can't be changed) tend to be more afraid of failure and see it not as an outcome but rather as an indicator of who they are. Those with a *growth* mindset (i.e., you can get better and "smarter" through effort) tend to view failures as more of a little bump in the road and know that if they put forth more effort and time, they'll get better. There is a plethora of information on how mindsets affect student learning and behavior available through books, articles, and websites. Dweck's book *Mindset: The New Psychology of Success* (2007) is a good place to start.

Offer Redos and Retakes

Why do we feel it's wrong to let kids have a second chance? How many of you passed your driver's test the first time? Don't adults have the opportunity to repeat tests such as for professional licensing? Don't authors write draft after draft prior to publishing a book? Then *always* make failure another chance to get it right.

In his article "Redos and Retakes Done Right," Rick Wormeli (2011) notes that "making students redo their learning until it meets high expectations demands far more of both students and teachers than letting them take a failing grade—but it also results in far more learning" (p. 24). Wormeli examines this idea and provides a solid rationale for permitting second chances in your classroom as well as practical tips for managing the process. For a more lighthearted but equally thoughtful look at how effective this approach is, read *Mr. DeVore's Do-Over: A Little Story for Teachers* (Puckett, 2005). This short, delightful, semi-autobiographical story illustrates how teachers can make a difference in a struggling student's life.

How students view and react to failure influences their attitude toward school, their interactions with others, and their behavior. Teaching students to cope with failure in a positive way will go far in building a classroom where students belong and result in a more peaceful and well-managed classroom.

Strategy 43: Question Your Questioning

There are lots of questions in teaching and learning—there certainly should be, anyway. Asking questions and seeking answers to questions is at the heart of learning. Questioning could be the most-used teaching strategy of all, as teachers ask dozens, maybe hundreds, a day. Dynamic, effective instruction is filled with good questions from teachers and students. Just asking questions is not enough, however; it is not a given that all questioning furthers learning. Educators need to take a thoughtful look at *why* they ask questions, *how* they ask questions, and *what kinds* of questions they ask. And then they must transfer what they know about questioning to the hands of students—to engage them fully as questioners in the classroom. Question your own questioning patterns in light of these three questions: Why? How? And what kinds?

Why Ask Questions?

When questions are asked in ways that enable students to contribute comfortably and confidently, and when the kinds of questions include a range of approaches from "closed" questions (those with yes/no or multiple-choice answers) and "open-ended" (those that encourage individual thoughts, conclusions, or viewpoints), the questioning process can

- Stimulate thinking at all levels, including higher-order skills.
- Spur students to reflect on ideas and information.
- Advance student understanding and achievement.
- Instigate student–teacher and student–student interaction.
- Invite students to an active role in learning.
- Ignite curiosity about a topic or concept.
- Review and summarize previous material.
- Solidify, deepen, and expand concepts introduced.
- Reveal what (and how) students are learning, thinking, and understanding.
- Help student and teacher assess progress.
- Model ways for students to ask their own questions.

How to Ask Questions

Teachers can ask students the most stimulating questions in the world, but if the questions are asked in ways that put students on the spot; intimidate them; expose their unpreparedness, indecision, or nervousness; or embarrass them in any way—all the value is lost. Worse, students will have been set back in their confidence and self-belief, security with the subject matter, and willingness to take risks. And belongingness will have taken a hit. Done thoughtfully and with the intent to show value and belief in each student, questioning can do the opposite. When students are able to engage in the question-and-answer process with positive outcomes, their sense of belonging gets a strong boost.

Consider these suggestions as you plan how to ask questions in your classroom.

Prepare students ahead of time for specific questions. Setting students up for success, particularly if a specific student has struggled in some way in your class, can be a great way to see what students really know. When time allows and it's reasonable to do so, spend some time with a student before or after school, during lunch, or at the end of class period to pre-teach the content you'll present to all students the next day. Listen to the questions the student asks. Once the student has an initial level of confidence regarding the content, help them develop a question or two to ask when the content is taught to the full class the next day. When you're teaching the content the next day, ask the student to do you a favor and ask the question in front of the class. This strategy helps build confidence for the struggling student and helps that student have additional time with content. One team of middle school teachers took this to another level and invited a small group of students to attend a 30-minute before-school "class" a few times a week to prepare them for upcoming content; students' confidence and understanding soared.

Take time for "wait time." Give students time to think. Wait time has a positive effect on learning (Brooks & Brooks, 2001). The foundational text *A Guide to Teaching Practice* recommends "waiting 3 to 5 seconds for closed questions and up to 15 seconds for open-ended questions" (as cited in Doherty, 2017).

Attend to the responses. Show enthusiasm about students' responses; engage with them. Ask a follow-up question, refer later to a student's answer, or ask others to think about and respond to the first response. Just as you pause after asking a question, include "wait time" before you move on to another student with another question. Never rush right on to the next question as if the first response were not important. Your response (verbal and nonverbal) is a great chance to afford dignity and importance to the student's answer and, thus, to the student.

Don't set a student up for failure. When you know a student has struggled with a specific topic or concept, don't put him on the spot in front of his peers by asking him a specific question you know he will not be able to answer. This adversely affects both classroom management and student dignity. When asking students questions, set them up for success by ensuring they're prepared for the question you are going to ask.

Randomly call on all students. Avoid calling on the same students most (or all) of the time while unintentionally overlooking quieter, passive, unsure, or bored students. Develop a method to keep track of whom you question when, ensuring all students are included and participate. You can pull popsicle sticks with students' names on them, call numbers assigned to students, or do "popcorn questioning." But this approach needs to be done in concert with not setting up students for failure; if you're using the popsicle sticks and pull the name of a student who would clearly struggle, call on another student. You can come back to the struggling student later, with an easier question. If you use a "no hands up" instruction, all students must be ready, because anyone could be asked to respond.

Say the name of the student *before* you ask the question. By getting the student's attention before you ask a question, you communicate that you really care about that student's answer and you want the student to listen carefully and think critically before answering the question. Randomly calling on the student after you ask the question can lead to embarrassment and potentially turn into classroom management problems if the embarrassed student acts out in response.

Vary the types of questions you ask. Questions can be teacher-made, student-made, or standardized. Using a variety helps keep students engaged and encourages them to think more critically. Student-made questions have the added benefit of helping students learn to develop and ask good questions while studying content.

Move from concrete to abstract. Because students in a class can vary greatly in their ability to understand abstract concepts, structure your questions to help students move from the concrete to the abstract. Beginning with some more concrete questions that have a more specific answer can help students feel more a part of the discussion and help avoid misbehavior because of "feeling dumb."

What Kinds of Questions to Ask

In his seminal work on classroom questioning, William W. Wilen (1991) reviewed the research on questioning practices. He found that the highest percentage of questions asked for factual information, and less than 20 percent required students to think. To teach well, teachers must use a mix of questions. Closed questions and open-ended questions both serve purposes. There are appropriate times at all grade levels for quick checks of information and facts. But teachers must include many (and a wide range of) questions that lead to deeper levels of thinking and expression of individual ideas.

When you ask questions that invite students' close examination and exploration, you are both promoting higher-order thinking skills and sending the message that you believe your students are capable of the cognitive processes for answering. You turn over control of the discussion to them—affording them independence and value. With open-ended answers, you invite them to share their voices, sending the message that you respect what they know and have experienced. Inviting student voice also communicates that you believe their ideas and opinions are important enough for everyone to hear. These signs of respect and belief are strong factors in belonging, which in turn can decrease classroom management problems.

The types of questions and sample prompts in Figure 6.2 can help you build a repertoire of questions that will foster critical thinking—both for yourself and to teach to your students. Apply these to topics, issues, debates, discussions, or investigations appropriate to your students' grade level.

FIGURE 6.2

Questions to Foster Critical Thinking

Ask questions that . . .	Sample prompts
Probe	What is going on here?
Challenge students to think deeply	What's behind this? What's missing in this description/argument/explanation? What more information do you need than is presented here?
Arouse students' curiosity and interests	What do you think will happen next? What would you need to do this/solve this?
Ignite creativity	Would the outcome be different if _____ were changed to ____? Is there a different way to look at/solve this? Where would you go to find answers to this question?
Spark connections between the topic and students' lives	If _____ is true, then what about _____? Where or when have you seen a similar situation/problem? When or where would this information be useful/harmful? What difference does this information make to you/to the world/to a particular group?
Establish an understanding of concepts	Why is someone making this statement/claim?
Encourage analysis and evaluation	Who is the audience for this information?
Apply concepts to different situations	How does this compare to _____? How would you apply _____ to _____?
Instigate discussion	Who believes this? What does the speaker/writer/creator believe? What do they want you to believe?
Stimulate more questions	What is the motive behind _____? What do you want or need to know about the source of this information?
Inspire students to reflect on their own responses and the responses of others	How do you know _____? What is the evidence for _____?
Call for interpretation (figuring out significance or relationships)	What's the point? Is this important? Why? Which of these is most influential/important/relevant/dangerous?

Why Do Students Need to Be Questioners?

We've given you some food for thought about your own questioning. Equally important is taking a close look at students' questions—and this may stretch your thinking even further than examining your own patterns.

Are your students asking questions? How often? Do you encourage them to question? Have you taught them how? Students should be asking *more* questions than teachers do. The same outcomes we previously described that happen when teachers ask questions will happen when students devise and ask their own questions and listen and respond to one another's questions. The results may be even more powerful. In Rosenshine, Meister, and Chapman's (1996) review of studies on student questioning, they point to substantial evidence that when students ask questions about content they are learning or something they have read, they make significant gains in understanding.

- **In the act of generating a question,** students must think about an idea and connect it to things they know or have recently learned. They need to call on previous knowledge and make sense of it in order to formulate a question.
- **In asking the question,** students have to articulate clearly what it is they are hoping to learn. In addition, asking questions engages them in a social connection with the listeners. This fosters maturity, autonomy, and courage.
- **In listening to the responses of others,** students have to analyze new information and integrate it into their thinking. This helps them expand upon previous knowledge. Sometimes it also helps students see what is missing in their own understanding.

When a student asks a question, the other students in the class are not only learning more about the topic at hand and gathering information that affects their own understanding but also getting a lesson in self-expression and social interaction. They're learning about how to ask and answer questions and how to give and receive feedback.

In an early study on questioning in science classrooms, researcher Glenn McGlathery (as cited in Barnette, 1994) reported that teachers asked about 50 questions in the average class period, whereas students were unlikely to ask even one. We'd wager that this still holds true, that teachers ask far more questions than students. As you polish your own skills, teach students the same understandings and strategies you need for yourself. Then step back enough to let them do plenty of questioning—of you and of one another. Enjoy the boon to student self-esteem, belief in their cognitive skills, and group connectedness.

Strategy 44: Give Feedback That Makes a Difference

If students are to improve, academically and behaviorally, they need honest, specific feedback that does not harshly judge and evaluate but rather encourages them to reflect on their work or their actions and think critically about how they can do better. Constructive feedback to students both promotes an individual's academic or personal growth and, at the same time, helps maintain a positive classroom environment. For feedback to make a difference, students should hear something specific, learn something from it that can be put into practice, and use it to do something better next time.

Be Private

Constructive feedback on student behavior and classwork is best given in private. Have quiet conversations with students during a work time, ask them to stay a few minutes after class, or set up a time for them to meet with you that works for both of you. Take this approach even if the feedback is positive; some students do not like to be singled out for any reason, and you may not ever see the behavior you were promoting again!

Be Specific

Don't just tell a student, "You did a good job in class today!" Specify the behavior or work you are complimenting. Did a student do a "good job" by staying seated during class, by not blurting out answers and interrupting others, or by not distracting other students by talking to them when other students were trying to listen? Instead, you might

- Describe the behavior objectively, focusing on the behavior, not the student: "When a question is asked or a comment is made in the middle of something I'm saying, ..."
- Describe the behavior's effect on others: "It's disruptive to the other students, and we all lose our train of thought."

- Provide the student with an alternative behavior or two: "When you have something to ask or share, please raise your hand and wait until I call on you" or "Why don't you write it down so you'll remember what it is you want to say when it's time for questions or comments?"

Give feedback to students as close to the action as possible. In research done on immediate versus delayed feedback, results indicated that students given immediate feedback have a greater increase in performance than those who receive it later (Kulik & Kulik, 1988).

Be Collaborative

Involve students in the process. Help them understand you are in this together and that you're there to support them in their efforts to do better in class. As principals, we've both found that open-ended questions work best when meeting with teachers after observing them in action. This approach has helped us avoid the trap of leading the teacher into saying what they think we want to hear. We've asked teachers questions such as "So how did you think your lesson went?" and followed up with such questions as "Why do you think that didn't [or did] work?" and "Is there an area you would like to improve upon?" and "How do you think the students felt about the lesson? What clues led you to that conclusion?" Letting teachers talk has given them—and us, as principals—more evaluative information and ideas for growth than would have been on the table if we had done all the "evaluative talking."

The more you can enable students to reflect on their actions, acknowledge where they might have done something differently, and suggest, themselves, something they can do to avoid the issue in the future, the better their progress will be.

Be Thoughtful

Too often what teachers perceive as good feedback that will lead to improvement has the opposite effect. When Patti was in junior high, she was overweight and not very physically adept. During a unit on gymnastics in PE, she struggled. But she did manage (with the help of friends) to learn how to do a backwards somersault on the balance beam. She was proud of herself—until the teacher remarked on how poorly she did, how she could never manage to pull herself up on the uneven parallel bars, and that she just needed to try harder to do better. What did she do? Patti vowed never to take another PE class that wasn't a requirement—and she didn't.

Be Calm

Responding to a misbehaving student with language that implies you are angry, disgusted, or fed up by their behavior is a surefire way to cut off communication and keep students from listening to what you have to say. Instead, stay objective and unemotional, and try the "sandwich" strategy: Describe any undesirable behavior between affirmations of positive behaviors:

- "I do enjoy having you in class and know that you're a good thinker and very interested in what we are learning." (positive)
- "However, several times today you inappropriately called out in the middle of our lesson, and that disrupted both me and the other students. I know that it's frustrating for you when you have your hand up and I don't call on you, but there are times I need to give everyone a chance to participate in the discussion." (undesirable)
- "I do appreciate your questions and contributions to our class discussions, and it's clear that you are a bright student. If I don't have that chance to call on you, you can always ask your question during our work time or after or before class." (positive)

Be Cautious

Know your students. Know if they respond better to private or public praise. Know if they need time to process before responding to feedback. Know that it is important to account for the cultural identity of the student and how that student might interpret what you say through the filters of cultural norms and past school experiences. Knowing how your students are likely to accept and respond to feedback will go a long way toward ensuring that your feedback will actually be helpful to them.

7

Belonging Thrives on Students Working Together

The best thing I've seen teachers do to help students belong is
to mix them into groups for learning together.

a 6th grader

*This chapter offers strategies for successful collaborative work and
ways to pass them on to your students. These include planning for
successful management, creating protocols for and with students,
teaching collaborative skills, reflecting on group work, and celebrating
both new learning accomplishments and increased belonging.*

Many teachers shy away from instruction that involves students working in
groups, fearing that the classroom will devolve into chaos. They worry that individual students will do too much of the work, too little of the work, or even none of
the work. They are unsure of how to assess a group project, especially if it appears
that only a few students worked hard on it. They envision behavior getting out of
control. They dread the clique-y conduct and picture kids being left out.

Unfortunately, by avoiding cooperative learning, teacher and students both
miss out on one of the most powerful learning strategies available in the classroom. They also bypass valuable opportunities proven to increase student belonging. It's true that all of those feared results can and often do happen when you send
kids off to work in groups. But disorder will not break loose when group work is

meaningful and properly planned, taught, and managed. So don't shy away from it. Learn how to do it well, and you'll delight in its benefits, which include helping students know and accept one another better and improving classroom management.

The terms *group work, cooperative learning,* and *collaborative learning* are often used interchangeably. Both cooperative learning and collaborative learning are instructional strategies in which a pair or small group of students "work together to maximize their own and each other's learning" (Johnson & Johnson, 2020, para. 5). Interdependence is a shared critical ingredient; students depend on one another for their own learning and the group learning. Usually, *cooperative learning* has a strong component of teacher direction in assigning tasks, monitoring the group, and contributing to assessment. *Collaborative learning,* on the other hand, is a form of cooperative learning in which students take more responsibility for structuring group efforts, deciding the tasks, finding source material, monitoring themselves, and assessing performance.

In this book, we use the term *cooperative learning,* a group-work strategy wherein the teacher has a strong role in the structure and process. When we mention *group work,* we are referring to *cooperative* group work. As *collaboration* is the act of working with someone else for the purpose of answering, producing, solving, or creating something, we will still use that term now and then, because students must collaborate when they tackle tasks in cooperative groups.

Cooperative learning offers an alternative to competitive or individualistic learning. It moves away from a passive approach to one where students are actively involved. Each individual is needed to make the group successful. Researchers use the term *positive interdependence* as a key ingredient for such group experiences; individuals only meet their goals when others in the group meet their goals, too (Pettigrew, 1998; Pettigrew & Tropp, 2008). The understanding is that each student in a cooperative group has a job: to carry out an equal part of the task, support and encourage other group members, and take responsibility for both individual and group outcomes, much like a team sport.

This instructional strategy goes beyond just gathering students together in a group. Cooperative learning involves specific structures to assure that all members play active, contributing roles. It is designed to make everyone in the group useful, important, valued, and affirmed—all of which contribute to belonging for every student and to positive classroom behavior.

Students with successful cooperative learning experiences make substantial growth in many academic, social, and emotional skills. When compared to competitive or individual learning, cooperative learning has been found to improve achievement, spark motivation, spur critical thinking, boost cognitive engagement, sharpen communication skills, raise student expectations for success, and increase individual responsibility and independence (Gillies, 2008; Gillies & Haynes, 2011; Johnson & Johnson, 1990, 2009; Johnson, Johnson, & Holubec, 2008; McCracken, 2005; Roseth, Johnson, & Johnson, 2008; Sapon-Shevin, 1994; Slavin, 1996).

Cooperative learning also has a powerful effect on student relationships. Joint communication, problem solving, and decision making lead to group members feeling more accepted and thus more willing to engage and help others. The more of these experiences that students have, the greater is the growth of caring relationships (Johnson & Johnson, 1990). In an early extensive study of cooperative learning research, Shelley Berman (1997) found that cooperative learning creates a bond that leads students to care about one another, develop prosocial behaviors, improve at solving social problems, contribute more to the well-being of others, and make decisions for the common good.

Well-managed group learning experiences also lead to harmony in the classroom and substantial growth in belonging. Cooperative learning is highly recommended as a prime strategy for increasing belonging, especially in settings with great diversity among students (Berman, 1997; Korinek, Walther-Thomas, McLaughlin, & Williams, 1999; McNamara, 1996; Osterman, 2000). In fact, Karen Bierman (2004), who studies peer rejection, found that positive interdependence (the key process in cooperative groups) helps to break down biases among diverse groups of students. She considers positive interdependence as *the only kind* of interaction that can motivate young people to rethink their previous conclusions about others. In their 2008 meta-analysis of studies on the effects of intergroup contact, Pettigrew and Tropp concluded that mixing members from different backgrounds into formalized groups (groups accountable to meet a particular purpose) increased empathy for, lessened anxiety around, and reduced prejudice toward people they would have previously avoided or rejected. Plus, experts have found that diverse groups come up with better ideas and get better results (Wells, Fox, & Cordova-Cobo, 2016).

Given the profound personal, social, and academic benefits, it is well worth the courage it takes for teachers to provide students with high-quality cooperative learning experiences.

Strategy 45: Craft a Winning Plan for Managing Groups

A management plan is essential to successful cooperative learning in your classroom; don't start group work without it. Badly managed group work will generate the opposite effects from what you want. It deteriorates your larger management picture and decreases belonging. Planned management—knowing what the purpose is and taking wise steps to reach it in an organized fashion—will help you and your students to reap all the benefits of cooperative learning.

Know that cooperative learning can be messy. Students might not be skilled at the process; every task is a little different; groups have different dynamics; collaboration is noisy and involves movement. If you honor the importance of structure and consistency (see Chapter 4), it will make everything happen more smoothly. We advocate a three-phase plan for organizing and managing collaborative groups in the classroom. As you see in Figure 7.1, it's a matter of *preparation, design*, and *delivery*.

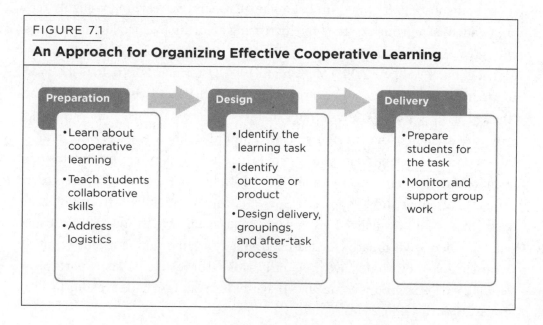

FIGURE 7.1

An Approach for Organizing Effective Cooperative Learning

Preparation
- Learn about cooperative learning
- Teach students collaborative skills
- Address logistics

Design
- Identify the learning task
- Identify outcome or product
- Design delivery, groupings, and after-task process

Delivery
- Prepare students for the task
- Monitor and support group work

Phase 1: Preparation

Your personal preparation needs will vary, of course, but the following actions are ones we recommend.

Learn about cooperative learning. If you're not experienced with group work, haven't felt comfortable or successful with past group work, or haven't gained any new cooperative learning ideas lately, spend some time searching out information and insights. Patti saw firsthand how well this worked when the health teachers at her school decided to use novels in literature circles to spark discussions on adolescent health issues and spent considerable time with the English teachers to learn the ins and outs of teaching and managing this type of collaborative learning experience.

Even if you've had success with cooperative learning in the past, it's worthwhile to review published research on the topic (see, for example, Johnson & Johnson, 1990, 2009, 2020; Johnson, Johnson, & Holubec, 2008; Kagan, 1988; McCracken, 2005), check out cooperative learning blogs, and talk with your colleagues about it.

There are dozens of reasons for group work—goals from simple to complex (e.g., exploring a new concept, reviewing already-learned information, practicing a process, learning about a new topic, brainstorming examples of a concept, organizing concepts, planning an inquiry, mapping out an argument). Some tasks are "closed" tasks you can use to check to see that students know certain information or can use a specific process. Others are "open-ended," with a variety of answers or interpretations. Use both types of tasks for cooperative learning.

Teach collaborative skills to students. Let students know what skills they'll need for successful cooperative group work. Weave instruction focused on these skills into topics you are teaching or planning to teach in any content area:

- **Communication:** active and respectful listening, contributing your own ideas, expressing claims and arguments (and backing them up with evidence), giving and receiving constructive feedback, paraphrasing and summarizing, asking questions
- **Interaction:** respectfully engaging with others' ideas and perspectives, ensuring everyone is included, flexibility, patience, managing behavior,

encouraging others and helping others succeed, reaching consensus, group decision making and problem solving, managing disagreements or conflicts

- **Organization:** meeting deadlines, taking responsibility for one's own work, approaches to brainstorming (e.g., "mind maps")

Whenever students begin to work in pairs or groups, do a quick a minilesson on one of the skills and make that a goal for the cooperative activity (along with the learning outcome). To teach a particular skill, describe and demonstrate specifics of how it looks or works in action, and ask students to describe or demonstrate them, too. Then practice. For example, "active and respectful listening" includes looking at the person talking and noticing how that person expresses an idea, noticing how others respond, listening and not interrupting, and being able to paraphrase the idea. (See Strategy 32, p. 101, for different ways to teach this particular skill.)

This is not a quick process; students will develop their collaborative abilities throughout their school years. Teach and build these skills over time. Practice and refine them until they become habits.

Address logistics. Successful collaborative group work has a lot of moving parts, from protocols (see Strategy 46, p. 157) to materials, space and time, and health and safety procedures. How do you want students to give feedback? How will you indicate start and stop time for the activity? As with any successful endeavor, thinking through all the moving parts before beginning will ensure a more positive outcome.

First, *consider the space and time* needed for your collaborative groups and their activities. Where will pairs or groups of students meet? This will vary according to the task (will they be making posters? rehearsing a demonstration?), length of the task, and size of the group. Try to envision scenarios for pairs answering questions about something they just read or heard, groups of four building a model, or groups rotating to interview other groups. Think about the physical arrangements, amount of room students will need to move, and how and when each group will move.

Obviously, the time requirement will vary with the task. You need to account for time to give directions and respond to student questions; face-to-face time in the groups; and group feedback, reflection, assessment, or goal setting. For some activities, groups will report back to a larger group. Not every one of these factors will play a part in every student-to-student learning activity, but if you enact a variety of such opportunities, chances are you'll encounter each of these needs.

In 2020, the COVID-19 pandemic made everyone focus on disease spread. Although there have always been communicable illnesses in schools, this experience left many teachers with a heightened awareness of health and safety. When planning group work or any activity that brings students in very close contact, think about this factor. Teach students behaviors that conform to your current health protocols. Keep this in mind when you choose strategies, add this consideration to your planning, and always encourage students to wash their hands regularly!

A word about noise: expect it. Group work can be loud. Be prepared to allow and encourage students to talk with one another. You want them to interact. Listen to the noise. If it's productive and on task, let it continue; if it's more social and off task or gets too loud, that's the time to intervene. Group work is interactive, so they'll need to talk, but there need to be times of quiet when work depends on individuals focusing on their own parts.

Phase 2: Design

A deliberate approach to the design of collaborative learning helps to ensure the work is worthwhile, orderly, and engaging. Here's what we recommend.

Identify the learning task. Some teachers start cooperative group work with a major long-term project that they think will lead to loads of learning and dynamite projects. It takes time and practice, however, to work up to doing this well and getting good results from and for students. Teaching collaboration takes a lot of scaffolding.

Our advice? *Start small.* Start with short tasks for pairs, teaching and practicing individual collaborative skills along the way. Put students in situations where success is guaranteed. Let them gain confidence in the process and comfort with one another. Progressively work toward more complex tasks. There is plenty of content that can be explored, reviewed, and deepened in small chunks. And, as they get more skilled, provide opportunities for groups to deal with less-than-successful situations (see Strategy 42, p. 135).

Next, *plan the details.* Think through all parts of it, from beginning to end. Ask yourself how the goal will be furthered by a cooperative approach. Don't force a task into a group format just for the sake of having students work in groups.

Identify the purpose of the group work—for yourself and for your students. They will need to know not only what they are to do but also why they are doing it. The following are characteristics of successful collaborative group tasks:

- The task can be broken down into equitable bites. If the bites are not the same for every group member, delegate who does which part. Be sure there is a job for each member.
- The task is interesting, engaging, and relevant for students.
- The task is both interdependent and independent, requiring members to work on their own but also to do some parts together and work for one another's success.
- The task has meaningful content that connects to what students are learning, already know, or need to learn.
- The task requires thinking and application of thinking. Aim to promote understanding.
- The task is worth doing; it has an important outcome. Make group work a little more challenging than what students can do on their own.
- The task has reasonable goals and expectations, and it can be completed in a reasonable amount of time.

At this point, *identify the intended outcome or product.* Your guidelines to students will need to be specific. For example, instead of telling students to "discuss this question," say something like this:

> Read the problem to yourself, twice. Think about how to solve it. Discuss your ideas with your partner and agree on two ways to solve the problem. On the paper, show—without using a spoken explanation—two different strategies you used to arrive at the solution.

This step is linked to logistics, in that you'll need to think about (and gather) materials that students require to complete the task. You also need to consider whether a task, particularly a longer one, needs a check-in during the process rather than waiting for completion. There will be situations in which it is helpful to students to have you do a quick review before they move on to the next step.

Design the delivery groupings and the after-task process. Considering all the decisions you've made so far in planning the task, decide how you will *explain the task to students* when you introduce it to them as well as what you will say at other times throughout the steps of the process (e.g., working, reflecting, evaluating, sharing). Write down what you plan to say. If the task is multistage or directions might be difficult to remember, put them in writing for the students. Short tasks—a question to answer, an idea to consider, a topic to gather opinions about—can be written on the board or projected on a screen.

You'll also need to *decide on the size of groups*. Smaller groups are often better for interdependent work; groups of two to four allow for more interaction, participation, and responsibility and lead to better learning outcomes (Kagan, 1988; Lou et al., 1996; Wilkinson & Fung, 2002). With slightly larger groups, you may be able to ensure greater diversity (Wilkinson & Fung, 2002), so do stretch to groups of four or five on occasion.

We recommend that you assign the groups, either composing them randomly (e.g., counting off numbers, grabbing a colored marble from a can) or with specific groupings in mind. The latter approach allows you to mix students to fit the needs of the task, avoid friends-only groups, and ensure students have opportunities to learn about, learn from, and work with students of differing abilities, perspectives, and backgrounds. It's important also to *design the after-task process*. How will students show their results? How will you assess outcomes? You need to identify the criteria by which products or group processes will be evaluated, plan a way for groups to reflect and give one another feedback, and choose how groups will share their outcomes or learn from other groups.

Finally, *review your plan!* Anticipate questions that students might ask and complications that may arise so you can be ready to handle them.

Phase 3: Delivery

It's go time. The third set of planning considerations covers ways to ensure the cooperative learning goes smoothly on the day it takes place by attending to the environment and interactions. We recommend the following actions.

Prepare students for the task. The environment for group work will be more comfortable and inclusive for students if they all understand the ground rules, structure, process, and expectations:

1. Have all the materials ready. If students need to bring materials to the group, ensure that they have access to the materials the activity requires and have those in hand before moving into groups.

2. Review the class agreements (protocols) for collaboration (see Strategy 46); these should be posted or projected. Explain that, although the task will give each group member one or more jobs, every person always has the job of keeping the agreements.

3. Explain the reasons for the task they'll be doing.

4. Identify the groups.

5. Send students to the location where they will be working. If students are new to one another or to group work, take a few minutes for students to introduce themselves or do a brief warm-up activity.

6. Once they are settled in groups (and only then), give clear directions for the task. Explain the expected outcome and how they are to get there. If you've put this in writing, go through it with them.

7. Let students know how long they have to work.

8. Talk about noise levels, if you plan for different noise levels. (Will there be time to work alone quietly *and* time to confer with group members?)

9. Find out if students understand the task: ask questions, randomly, that prompt them to repeat or summarize the directions. Give students a chance to ask questions.

10. Get started!

Monitor and support group work. As students go about the task, continue to play an active but nonintrusive role. This means you need to *stay present* and move occasionally among the groups; pay attention to how they're doing, but don't hover. This will give you a chance to *observe both group processes and individual engagement*. A few dos and don'ts about that:

- DO be available to answer questions—but only when asked.
- DON'T intervene unless absolutely necessary. Behave as if you believe they can do the task on their own and work out their own questions or difficulties.
- DO intervene if it helps a group member who's struggling with collaborative processes or belongingness.

When the groups have completed their task, *give instructions for the next step*. This might be answering a reflection question, sharing their outcome with the pair next to them, posting a visual record on the wall, and so on. Be sure to give a separate direction for each step that is part of the process you've designed, whether reflecting and sharing reflections, evaluation of their work against the criteria, feedback, or sharing with the wider group. And, with each direction, give students time to think (if needed) before doing the action—and time for them to do the action before you give the next direction.

Reinforce positive collaboration by giving students some sort of affirmation about their work before sending the groups back to their seats (or wherever you want them to head). We advise taking a few minutes to *debrief the activity* with the class, soliciting input on what went well and what didn't. And on that note, always *reflect on the process:* find time to make notes about what you learned from watching the group work and from listening to students' feedback. It's how you'll continue to improve your practice and their learning.

Strategy 46: Agree on Student Protocols for Collaboration

We've both worked in settings with leaders who assumed that, because we were teachers, we automatically knew how to work in groups. We would inevitably get into groups and find that everyone had a different idea about how things should work. Or we'd dive into promoting our own ideas and not even think about group processes. With no protocols to follow for group work, a lot of time is wasted spinning wheels, not knowing how to function as a team—time that should be spent accomplishing tasks.

Students should have many varied experiences working collaboratively for many different purposes related to academic tasks and other processes in classroom life. But just as school leaders assume teachers know how to work in groups, many teachers assume the same about their students (particularly those in older grades). Don't take this for granted! Such an assumption can wreak havoc on classroom management and negate all the benefits of group work.

For your plan for how you will launch and manage group work (see Strategy 45) to be effective, you also need a guide for students to use every time they work cooperatively—and your students should be involved in designing these protocols. Talk with students about their past experiences with groups; try to glean what they think worked or did not work. How do the individual students in your class understand and engage with group work and collaboration? Get students involved in generating, discussing, adding to, or adapting the set of protocols for effective group work.

The word *protocol* means "an agreement"; it is generally used to describe a group of behaviors expected in a certain situation. Students can decide on how to label these guidelines (e.g., "Agreements for Collaboration," "Our Collaboration Code," "Rules of Engagement," "Ground Rules for Group Work," "Group Work Protocols"). Whatever the title, set guidelines, put them in writing, and get them into students' hands (and posted on the wall of your classroom). Then teach students how to do each part of the agreement.

Committing to Group Protocols

Figure 7.2 is a sample student agreement for working in cooperative groups. We suggest that, once the class understands and endorses the protocols, any written list be signed by each student. This begins the process of individual ownership of roles and responsibilities in whatever pair or group the student joins in the future.

FIGURE 7.2

Template for a Student Collaboration Agreement

In working on a task with other students, I agree to

- Come to the group prepared with all necessary materials.
- Look directly at the person talking and listen thoughtfully.
- Show respect for everyone's ideas and seek to understand the perspective of others.
- Participate equally with thoughtful, respectful ideas and questions.
- Take my turn talking (and not interrupt another speaker).
- Do my best to help everyone have equal time to give ideas and ask questions.
- Explain reasons or evidence for any answer, suggestion, or argument that I put forth.
- Take responsibility for finishing my equal part of the work, on time, without being reminded.
- Take responsibility for helping others succeed with their work.
- Take responsibility for managing myself.
- Give meaningful, useful feedback to other group members.
- Take part in solving problems or resolving conflicts.
- Help and encourage others in the group.
- Stay with my group during work time.
- Frequently rate myself on how well I hold to these agreements.

Signature: _____ Date: _____

Tips for Teaching Protocols

Define the terms and discuss their meanings with students. The literal definitions of *cooperation* and *collaboration* are generally similar—or even identical: they both define the action or process of working together to meet the same goal, which may be the creation of a product. *Cooperative learning* is the process of working with someone else, not just to produce something but for the purpose of understanding, answering, solving, producing, or creating something in order to learn. Its value stretches far beyond the task of working side by side to get something done. Cooperative groups are based on *interdependence*. This means that, to do the task, each student's success is dependent on every other student's success.

Discuss with students the foundations of collaboration. The collaborative process is based on these understandings and beliefs:

- Each member is equally valuable to the group.
- We will be successful only by working together. Each of us is responsible for the success of the group and the success of each member of the group.
- Each person is committed to finishing the task and doing it well.
- We are each accountable for our own learning.
- Each person is responsible for the well-being of the other group members. We should ensure each member feels genuinely included, respected, supported, and comfortable.
- We are committed to using our best skills of communication, problem solving, and conflict resolution.
- The process of working together and learning from one another is just as important as the final answer or product.

Model the protocol for students. In Strategy 45, we recommend teaching collaborative skills before bringing students into group work. It's essential for students to know what those skills—listening thoughtfully, asking questions, giving helpful feedback, participating equally—*look like* in the context of group work.

- Let students see you following the jointly created ground rules. Make sure that they see you keeping to the agreements—in your behavior with them and in your behavior with colleagues and other groups.
- Arrange for students to practice the protocol often, throughout the school year. Sometimes teachers teach a skill or process and think it has "stuck." Each new group experience presents different ways to apply the protocols. Take time to re-examine and strengthen these habits.
- Affirm examples. When you see students having success with co-designed protocols, collaborative processes, and cooperation skills, say so—and encourage students to do the same. Encourage group pride for tasks that go well.

Strategy 47: Untangle a Problem, Together

You can start the "conversation" about collaboration early in the school year, with an activity that plunges students into the mode of working together while at the same time giving them a fun, active challenge. The goal of this kind of activity is to inspire and prepare students for "untangling" different sorts of problems, in different content areas, together—and it sets the stage for learning about the process of collaboration.

A Physical Untangling

The "Gordian knot" dates back to stories of Alexander the Great and refers to a complex, challenging puzzle or problem. In its commercial forms, the Gordon knot game is a hard "take-apart" puzzle with many steps to the solution. In our version, groups of six to eight students actually create their own knots, and then each group works together to untangle a knot made by another group. With this activity, expect some commotion—along with plenty of creativity, social interchange, and problem solving. It's a cost-effective activity, too; all you need is space and three- to four-foot lengths of rope (e.g., cotton clothesline rope; one cord for every two people in a group).

Step 1: Form the groups. The number must be even. If that is not possible, have some students serve as process observers and rotate in during a second round. Each group should form a standing circle. Give the appropriate number of ropes to each group.

Step 2: Students in each group form a wheel—and then a knot. Students standing directly across from each other hold ends of one cord, so that all cords cross at the same point in the middle. On your signal, students must create a big messy "knot" in the center by walking and twisting and moving around. As the knot gets bigger, there will be less rope for them to hold on to. Stop the groups when they only have about 18 inches or so left. Ask them to carefully set the knot on the floor with the spokes coming out from the center.

Step 3: Groups rotate and untangle the knots. Rotate the groups so that each is no longer with its original knot. (If you have any students who did not participate in the first steps, they might change places with students who did, and those students are now observers.) Students in each group should pick up the new knot and try to untangle it.

Step 4: Discuss the experience. When all groups have finished, take a short break to calm down and gather to discuss the experience. You can give the groups discussion questions in writing or pose them one at a time, asking students to come to consensus about one or two answers for each question:

- What were the hardest parts of this?
- What worked well?
- Was it easier to create or untangle the knot?
- What would you do differently next time?
- What did you learn about working on this problem as a group that you can apply to the next group problem or task?

Give each group a turn to share some of their answers. As an alternative, you can do this step as a whole class. (If some students watched the process, ask them to share their observations first or save their comments until after students have talked.) You may want to keep a record of some of the suggestions they give for future group work and incorporate those into future plans for collaboration.

Variations of this game include the "human knot game" (where each student holds the hands of two other students, and the group tries to untangle itself without letting go of hands) and the "silent knot game" (doing the activity without speaking). With either variation, discuss the challenges, successes, and unique problems posed by that method.

A "Mental-Only" Untangling Alternative

Out of consideration for students who may not be comfortable with the degree of physical closeness the previous activity requires—or just for variety—consider the Lock-in Survival Puzzle.

Put students in groups of five to eight and present this scenario:

It's Friday afternoon, and you have just been locked in the classroom until Monday morning. You cannot pick the door's lock, break the door down, or break a window to escape. You're stuck here over the entire weekend. You have 30 minutes to agree upon 10 items that you will need in order to survive. Once you have come to an agreement on the 10 items, rank them in order of importance. Your goal is for everyone to agree on the 10 items and their ranking in the next 30 minutes.

Debrief by holding a class discussion asking questions such as the following, adapted as needed to suit the age of your students:

- How did you come to an agreement on the items you would need?
- Was it easier agree on the items or the ranking of the items?
- What problems did you encounter?
- What might have made the process easier?
- What did you learn that will help simplify making group decisions in the future?

Strategy 48: Fire Up Collaboration with Lively Strategies

Once you have a management plan and established protocols for students, what type of collaborative tasks will you assign them? The tasks need to be meaningful, challenging, and achievable; they also need to spark students' attention and invite them into a group venture.

The strategies in this section promote belonging and improved classroom management. They work across all content areas and with many age groups. Although most are fairly simple, they are not just for beginners, and each can be applied to tasks of different complexity levels and used again and again throughout the year. Each time you provide students with the opportunity for collaboration, you are also providing them with an opportunity to practice their self-management skills.

Think-Pair-Share

Give students a topic, question, claim, or idea to define, answer, take a position on, or decide. Read the question or statement to the whole class or ask student pairs to read it together. Then pause; give everyone at least a full minute to think and jot down a definition, opinion, or other idea for an answer. Then, in each pair, Student A states and briefly explains the idea or answer. Student B paraphrases what was heard. After switching roles, each pair shares their ideas or answers with the class.

Think-Pair-Share-Square and **Two-Four-Eight** extend this approach. For the first, after the two students have had an opportunity to discuss the concept, combine two pairs into a group of four. This group shares and discusses ideas and arrives at a group consensus as to an answer or decision. For the latter, first ask pairs to agree on, for example, a definition of a word. Combine two pairs into a group of four, which should craft an agreed-upon definition. Then combine two fours into a group of eight; again, they work to reach consensus about a definition. Ask one person from each group of eight to share the group's definition with the class. As a whole class, discuss what the definitions have in common and how they differ. Depending on the task, you may want to decide upon one definition to be used for the class.

Get Up and Go

This strategy allows for students to hear several different opinions or perspectives on a topic. Have students sit in one large circle facing one another. Have them discuss a topic or answer a question with the person sitting to their right or left. Then, have all students whose birthday is in March—or who have a dog, or who are wearing tennis shoes, or some other commonality—stand up and get ready to "get up and go." Those standing will move to a seat left vacant by someone else who is also standing. You can use this strategy multiple times during a discussion, with different students moving each time based on different criteria, allowing students to communicate with many different partners throughout the discussion. When each student has heard several perspectives, gather students into groups of three or four. Each group shares the answers they heard and arrives at a consensus of one or two of the most convincing or compelling. These can be shared, then, with the larger group.

Gallery Walk

This is a good way to encourage positive feedback and acknowledge the contributions of others. Although we'll use an example of students defining a value, "accountability," this activity can be used with any content question or topic. Form groups of four. Give each group two blank posters and a marker (a different color for each group) and have them write *YES* at the top of one and *NO* at the top of the other. In their groups, students brainstorm examples of what accountability looks like—and does not look like—in practice (i.e., how can you tell someone is behaving with accountability? How can you tell that someone is not behaving with accountability?). Students write their examples on the posters. Mount the posters on the walls, with space between the pairs of posters.

Each group takes a turn standing by their charts and explaining their choices. After eliminating repeated examples, one or two students transfer the remaining examples to one summarizing poster. On a signal from the teacher, groups move around the "gallery." Group members put stars by examples they feel are most important or relevant and questions by examples they don't completely understand. One person from each group shares the items that were starred and answers any of the questions asked for the rest of the class.

Snowball Fight

Writing something on paper, wadding it into a "snowball," and throwing it to another class member is a fun way to work together. This is a good strategy, but it takes planning to ensure the activity doesn't get too chaotic!

Everyone must agree to the basic ground rules. Remind students before beginning a snowball fight that they shouldn't run or yell (but show some grace when they do if it's not intentional and is just excitement). Set guidelines about the force with which they can throw; ask them to toss a paper "snowball" in the air and let it fall; that's the velocity to aim for.

Have every student write down a question they have about a concept they have been learning; you may provide a list of questions for them to choose from or simply ask them to come up with their own questions. When you give a signal, students wad the sheet of paper on which they've written their question into a ball and have a group snowball "fight." When you tell them to stop, students pick up the closest snowball and write down an answer or a few thoughts about the question on the paper they hold. If you think it will work, you can then hold another short "fight," call time, and have everyone pick up a paper. Gather students into groups of four or five to share the questions and answers. End by having each group reach a consensus about a key idea they learned or an unanswered question they have.

One-Minute Papers

After a lesson or other activity where students learn content, give students a question to answer about the content. It can be a question with a specific answer (e.g., "What are the stages in the life cycle of a caterpillar?" "What was the central problem in the story you just read?" "How does photosynthesis work?"), or it can be more open-ended (e.g., "What is the most beneficial thing about the internet?" or "Where would you use the information we learned from the video we just watched?"). It may be a question that requires students to reflect on what they learned or understood (or did not understand) about content just presented (e.g., "What is the most important thing you learned doing this lesson?" or "What didn't you quite understand?"). Tell students they will have one minute to write a paper that answers the question. Give them a minute to think and a minute to write.

When the writing stops, combine students into pairs or groups of three. Give students time to share their responses with each other. If the question had a specific answer, ask groups to arrive at a clear consensus answer. If the task involved open-ended questions, you might ask groups to compose a statement of a key idea or come to consensus on a question they need to have answered.

Jigsaw

In the jigsaw strategy, each member of a small group becomes an expert on a particular aspect of a topic or problem. Break up the content from a topic into learning sections. Send one member from each jigsaw group (usually three to five students) to a different "expert" group to explore one of the content parts. In the "expert" groups, students work together to learn the content material well—well enough to teach it comfortably and confidently to the others in their home group.

The "experts" return to their home jigsaw groups, which are groups of experts on different parts of the overarching topic. Each expert takes responsibility for teaching their part of the "puzzle" to the rest of the group, until the group puts the whole "puzzle" of the content together.

In this activity, all students have two group experiences: They first learn with and from a number of others and cooperate to learn something new well enough to teach it. Then, they have an opportunity to teach what they know to others and listen to what others in their "jigsaw" group can teach them. This generates a lot of thinking, communicating, and synthesizing *together*—all while relying on one another to complete both the tasks of learning and teaching.

Strategy 49: Make Group-Work Reflection a Habit

Reflection practices are an important part of the learning process because they help individuals analyze their (academic and behavioral) strengths and needs and set goals to improve. Similarly, reflections on work done together can help students gain a better understanding of group processes and their individual contributions to the group, including how their own actions furthered or hindered the group's work. This process is an excellent experience in formative assessment—one that benefits both students and teacher.

Tips for Managing Group Work

As with any part of the group-work process, the reflection or evaluation stage needs teacher direction. It will only be successful if this, like other steps, is managed well. You will need to guide students through the process until they're skilled at doing it. Even then, you must be an active part of monitoring. Self-assessment and group assessment aren't matters of telling students to "Evaluate your part in the group work" or "Talk with your group about how the experience worked." In planning for cooperative learning groups,

- Set clear goals for the task (see Strategy 45, p. 150). Make sure students have a clear understanding of what is expected. They can't reflect at the end of the task unless they know what they were expected to do during the task.
- Choose appropriate tools or activities for reflection—ones that include criteria or guidelines for reflection—and teach students to use them. Tools for reflection on collaborative experiences should be appropriate for your students' age, their level of experience with cooperative activities, and the specific task to be done. Scoring guides, checklists, or other formats used early in the year may be fairly simple; later in the year, more complex methods can be used.
- Share the reflective method with students and have them practice it.
- Have students share or discuss their reflections. It's important for them to review these before the next collaborative experience. Encourage them to point out what they want the others or you to know that should be celebrated and what could be changed or improved for the next group task.
- Take notes on what you learn. This process is instructive for both teachers and students.

The reflection process has a significant effect on students' sense of belonging. In this situation, they take risks to write down and name their accomplishments and speak them out loud. They share their successes and not-quite-successes. They expose their needs. In evaluating the group-work process, they get the chance to affirm and further bond with their group members. But they also have to be brave enough to reveal their thoughts about what did not go so well. *This experience of reflecting is the part of group work where students get to know one another best.* It is a growth-producing, relationship-building process. Equal sharing of reflections, managed well and in a safe setting, brings students closer and increases their feeling of belonging.

You can show students that the feedback they bravely put forth is important by paying attention to what they teach you about their group experiences. Listen to their reflections and ask follow-up questions. Use the information to help you assess areas of group-work strengths as well as skills that may need more instruction.

Managing the Reflection Process

Templates (see Figures 7.3 and 7.4) can help manage the reflection process. They serve as guides for the task of revisiting or evaluating what they've done in their

FIGURE 7.3

Template for Individual Reflection on Collaborative Work

Name _____ Date _____

Group task _____

	Strongly agree	Agree	Some-what agree	Disagree
I completed all the tasks for which I was responsible on time.				
I contributed positively and usefully to our group.				
I did my very best work.				
I worked well with the other group members.				
I was a good listener and didn't try to take over the group.				
I respected the ideas and contributions of others in the group and gave them helpful feedback.				
I worked with others to solve problems as they arose.				
I was flexible and willing to change things when necessary.				
I did my fair share of the group's work.				
Other group members would say I was a good member of the group.				
Here's what I did especially well:				
Here's what I need to improve:				
The most important thing I learned from others in my group was . . .				

FIGURE 7.4

Template for Group Reflection on Collaborative Work

Students in the group _____

Group task _____ Date _____

	All of the time	Some-times	Rarely	Not very often
We finished our task on time.				
Everyone contributed to the project.				
We did the very best work we could.				
We cooperated with one another.				
We helped one another when needed.				
We shared ideas, discussed them, and came to an agreement.				
No one tried to take over the group.				
We were flexible and willing to change things when necessary.				
Everyone did their fair share of the group's work.				
We were good teammates.				

The best part of working together was . . .

Something we could have done better was . . .

Something we learned that we all agree was important:

groups. You want students to reflect on their own participation in group work, and you also want groups to reflect together on their process and accomplishments. Reflection forms should provide students with a set of criteria for evaluating how they did. When your students know what to do every step of the way, and when you are monitoring their work, the process is more likely to go smoothly. Note that the group reflection is, itself, a collaborative experience; individual members are not assessing the group.

If your students are collaborating frequently (as they should be), you don't need to ask for lengthy or time-consuming reflections every time; that would become burdensome. For brief collaborations, just sharing with a partner or jotting down a "note to self"—one thought, one thing done well, one goal for next time—is enough. When you do ask students to reflect in a written form, keep these reflections for future reference. A series of self-reflections can allow students to see progress in their collaborative skills.

Individual reflections (Figure 7.3) may also serve as the basis for a conversation within the group or individually with the teacher. Group members can use their group reflection (Figure 7.4) as the basis for a discussion, or they can collaborate and agree on responses together. With younger or inexperienced students, you may wish to guide the discussion, allowing time for each individual to contribute.

Strategy 50: Celebrate Group Belonging

Collaborative groups rely on interdependence. Every group member is responsible for the success of every other group member and for the success of the group as a whole. Talk about belonging! There is hardly a better way to feel useful and important—to be somebody—than to be recognized as integral to the group's success. Good-quality cooperative learning reminds both teacher and students that *everybody in the group is somebody*. A class in which everybody (including the teacher) feels like somebody is much easier to manage than a classroom with one or more members who feel like nobodies.

Renowned cooperative-learning researcher Robert Slavin (1991) highlighted research findings "that people who cooperate learn to like each other" (p. 96). In the years since Slavin's work, many research studies have affirmed that this is a prime benefit of cooperative learning: It promotes interpersonal relationships among students, including those with different learning needs, social and behavioral challenges, and cultural or ethnic backgrounds (Gillies, 2014).

We've chosen to complete our book with a strategy that brings students together to collaborate in order to celebrate belonging. We urge you to make celebration a regular part of group work. Individual groups should celebrate accomplishments, successful work processes, new insights and skills, their relationships, and the satisfaction of completing a task. The entire class should also be acknowledged for its growth in collaborative group work, not just after finishing a big group project but for an accumulation of many tasks. Celebrate progress, commitment to tasks, productive cooperation, mutual kindness, and the wonderful new concepts your students have helped one another learn. Here are a few suggestions for the forms that celebration can take.

Belonging Puzzles

When they create these puzzles, students will

- Increase belonging by working on a group task about belonging.
- Gather different viewpoints so that every student hears every other student's perspective, experience, and ideas.
- Honor the voice of every group member.

- Collaborate on a meaningful task that includes thinking about the value of one another.
- Produce a final, joint product that summarizes personal belonging beliefs and experiences.
- Reflect on their group-work journey, together.

Step 1. Start with groups of four or five students. Ideally, these would be groups that have worked together previously, perhaps recently having completed a somewhat complex project. Give each group a piece of posterboard (a different color for each group, if possible). Groups will also need scissors, pencils, pens, and colored markers.

Step 2. Instruct students to label the poster (in any orientation) with the word *Belonging* and to design and decorate that side of the poster however they like. Their posters can have images and blocks of color but no words other than the label. The group can choose a plan for how they will do this and how members contribute equally.

Step 3. When the decoration is complete, instruct students to get ready to turn the poster into a jigsaw puzzle. Drawing puzzle pieces on the blank side of the posterboard with light pencil lines is one way to do this. A group's puzzle must have twice the number of pieces as the number of group members. Encourage them to keep the pieces of similar size—no matter what the shape. Let them know that they'll be writing on the pieces, so the pieces shouldn't be too small or skinny. When they've sketched out their pieces, they can cut their puzzles.

Step 4. Now it's time for labels on the puzzle pieces. Half of the pieces will each have a question. You can type these on paper, cut them out, and give them to students to glue on the puzzle piece, or students can write them on the pieces. Make sure students understand that each group member will write an answer to the question—so the question itself should take up only enough room to be clear and readable. Here are some sample questions:

- How does working in groups help students feel a sense of belonging?
- What is the best thing this group has done to help you feel that you belong?
- What is the best thing you have done to help yourself belong to the group?
- If a sense of belonging is not felt by everyone, what happens to the group and its work?
- How does belonging help to create a class setting where the groups and individuals can work without disruptions and misbehavior?

Step 5. Each group member writes an answer to one of the questions. Answers do not have to be complete sentences but must be complete enough to make the point. Puzzle pieces are then passed around the circle until every member has added their answer to each question. The group sets these puzzle pieces aside for now.

Step 6. Groups distribute the remaining puzzle pieces among their members; students write their names on their pieces. Then, direct them to finish this statement: "A valuable skill, lesson, or improvement that I have gained from working in this group [working in groups] is _____." Let students know that the answers should not take up all the space, because other group members will be writing on their puzzle piece.

Step 7. Instruct students: "Look at each of the group members, one at a time. Think about what that person has contributed to the group. Think about their special skills, attitudes, or ways of relating to others that you've noticed have helped make others in the group succeed or feel comfortable in the group." Students pass their signed puzzle pieces to the right. Give a couple of minutes for students to write their thoughts about the person whose name is on the puzzle piece received. Students can choose to add their names to their comments—or not. Then repeat this process until every group member has made a comment about every other member.

Step 8. Each group mixes up all the pieces. Then at your signal, groups put their puzzles together. Give students time to look over their finished puzzles— and those of the other groups—and take part in whatever conversation naturally develops. If conversations are slow to start, you could jump-start that process by asking or having some questions on the board such as "What did you find most interesting about this process?" "What surprised you?" or "What did you learn about your classmates?"

Step 9. End the activity with a whole-group celebration of group work that has increased belonging. Surprise students with an ice cream party, extra socialization time, a funny video, or some other unexpected reward.

The Power of the Pen

Students recognizing one another for their accomplishments and actions is a very powerful way to build belonging. This recognition gives something to students that adult compliments can't ever supply. Encourage students to give and get this kind of connection and affirmation.

We've seen this activity carried out in all kinds of ways. Some teachers ask each student to write their name at the top of a blank piece of paper. The papers are then passed around the room, with each student writing a compliment to the student whose name is on the top of the page. Other teachers have students tape a blank piece of paper to their back and ask the class to silently walk around the room and write a compliment on each student's paper.

Just before the long winter break, Laurie's daughter's high school Spanish teacher asked each student to type a positive statement about every other student in the class, using a Google Form. The teacher compiled all statements anonymously and gave a paragraph of statements to each student before the break. Laurie's daughter Emma loved reading the comments, and so did her parents. It certainly spiked belonging for her. What a positive, affirming way to send students off on a break! And what an uplifted spirit accompanied those students when they returned to school.

Conclusion:
On the Belonging Journey

In early 2016, we saw the first sparks of our fire for belonging. We sat in our favorite café in Laurie's hometown of Whitefish, Montana, warming our hands around cups of cappuccino while the January snow swirled over the shores of Whitefish Lake. Patti had traveled from Oregon for a weekend to huddle together with Laurie around a new idea for a book.

For several weeks, we'd been asking ourselves and each other just what it was that lay at the foundation of the schools we administered and other schools we had helped to improve. Both of us had worked for years to build school cultures with academic excellence and social supports that would enable students to thrive as whole persons. We could recite in our sleep the factors key to school improvement and success. But what was the thread that tied together the needs of students and the effective programs and practices for a whole school community? What was it, really, that inspired students to *want* to come to school, to achieve their best once they got there, to get along with one another, to believe that they could learn, and to take responsibility for their behavior and their learning? What was it, for that matter, that inspired *us* (teachers and administrators) to those same ends?

We'd made lists and written paragraphs and batted around ideas in many discussions on our phones and digital devices. On that snowy day, however, we were struck by the number of times the word *belonging* had come up in our conversations. We realized that all the things we wanted for kids could happen only when they felt they belonged.

Starting then, we retuned our radars to the connections among belonging and all the elements of successful schools. These discoveries led us to write a book with a belonging theme and to subsequently share it in seminars, webcasts, and training sessions. We ran into teachers who were as excited as we were about belonging and who were hungry to learn more about how to make it happen. They asked plenty of questions about how to establish classrooms with goals of increasing belonging.

It was requests from these teachers that brought us to examine and write about what we were realizing was a natural (and powerful) connection between belonging and classroom management. Strengthening the sense of belonging for members of the school community and getting a handle on consistent, positive (and effective) classroom management—these are two imperative needs for every educator. When you improve one, you uplift the other.

We're thrilled to continue on this adventure of propagating belonging. We want to encourage you to understand that belonging isn't a final destination but an ongoing journey. We hope that all students and staff members gain greater senses of belonging—to the point where they value themselves, enter classrooms with comfort and not fear, learn well, and love to come to school. But belonging is more like the vehicle in which you travel than it is like the final stop; you need to keep it fueled, polish it up, keep it running smoothly, and (sometimes) repair it. We can say the same about good classroom management. It, too, needs ongoing vigilance, care, and periodic fixing.

We want to encourage you as you continue *your* "belonging" journey. Work on both belonging and classroom management can and should meld with what you already do. Belonging is not a new content area. It plays a part in any content you teach; it is already a factor of every moment of classroom life. You just need your new understandings and strategies to turn belonging from an "issue" into a gift that helps students feel, learn, and behave better. Management, too, is already happening. Most teachers are working on it regularly. This is just a bit of a twist: to look at management through the lens of belonging.

At the beginning of this book, we asked you to reflect on the duo of belonging and classroom management, on your own belonging, and on the current belonging practices you employ. Revisit these reflections as you keep working toward a more belonging-centered way of classroom management.

We know teaching and managing a class can be challenging, difficult, and daunting. We've been there. But we also believe that this passionate mission is extremely important. Nothing leads to that feeling of accomplishment like a student making a change for the better, having a student come back years later to thank you for the difference you made in his life, opening a thank-you note quietly left on your desk, or receiving a phone call from a parent telling you of the tremendous influence you've made in her child's life. Never underestimate the difference you can make in the lives of your students by helping them belong.

The more you attend to the belongingness of those around you, the more you'll grow in your ability to foster belonging. The more the members of your classroom belong, the smoother classroom management will be. The better the classroom management is, the greater the boost to belongingness. It's a beautiful cycle of community creation and growth. We can guarantee that all your efforts will be worth the courage and work you put into them. Celebrate the belonging gains you see in yourself, your students, and your colleagues. Celebrate, too, the comfort and safety of a well-managed, belonging-centered classroom.

We'll leave you with the words of a middle school student friend of Laurie's daughter, who was asked, "Why does it matter to have a sense of belonging at school?" This was the reply:

> Without a sense of belonging, you are empty. Belonging is absolutely necessary for your overall happiness, self-esteem, and mental health. It affects everything! It affects your motivation to do anything.

Acknowledgments

We have leapt into another project together—a book on a topic for which we share a deep passion. How much more enjoyable it is to do this writing with support from others who are equally passionate about belonging!

"Thank you" and a simple acknowledgment does not seem quite enough for Marjorie Frank, our friend and colleague who has served as a highly talented consultant and editor on three separate projects now. Marj sees the big picture, understands the value that educators bring to their work each day, and shares her talents widely to continue to give back to the field.

We would like to offer a special thank-you to our educator colleagues and friends Erin Scholes and Carrie Wick, who helped review content and provided suggestions, thoughtful insights, and encouragement. And our deepest appreciation also goes to Cossondra George—not only for sharing valuable feedback on an earlier draft but also for writing a thoughtful foreword.

As teachers and administrators throughout our adult lives, our work with Talent Middle School in Oregon, Smokey Road Middle School in Georgia, and Evergreen School District in Montana has helped mold us into the educators we are. We are extremely grateful to the colleagues, students, parents, and community members who have worked alongside us; their influences on our growth, much of our work, and this book are immeasurable.

Finally, thank you to the friends and family who continue to support our desires to work hard and play hard. Laurie extends special thanks to her husband, Daniel, and daughter, Emma, for affirming her in following her passion and for reminding her to stay grounded. Patti thanks her husband, Dan, for supporting and encouraging her to continue doing the work she loves.

References

Akey, T. M. (2006, January). *School context, student attitudes and behavior, and academic achievement: An exploratory analysis.* MDRC. Retrieved from https://www.mdrc.org/sites/default/files/full_519.pdf

Alexander, K., Entwisle, D., & Horsey, C. (1997). From first grade forward: Early foundations of high school dropout. *Sociology of Education, 70*, 87–107. doi:10.2307/2673158

Allen, K. A., & Bowles, T. (2012). Belonging as a guiding principle in the education of adolescents. *Australian Journal of Educational & Developmental Psychology, 12*, 108–119.

Allen, K. A., Kern, M. L., Vella-Brodrick, D., Hattie, J., & Waters, L. (2016). What schools need to know about fostering school belonging: A meta-analysis. *Educational Psychology Review, 30*(1), 1–34. doi:10.1007/s10648-016-9389-8

Ames, C. (1992). Classrooms: Goals, structures, and student motivation. *Journal of Educational Psychology, 84*, 261–271. doi:10.1037/0022-0663.84.3.261

Anderman, E. M. (2002). School effects on psychological outcomes during adolescence. *Journal of Educational Psychology, 94*(4), 795–809. doi:10.1037/0022-0663.94.4.795

Anderman, L. H. (2003). Academic and social perceptions as predictors of change in middle school students' sense of school belonging. *Journal of Experimental Education, 72*, 5–22. doi:10.1080/00220970309600877

Anderman, L. H., & Freeman, T. M. (2004). Students' sense of belonging in school. In P. R. Pintrich & M. L. Maehr (Eds.), *Advances in motivation and achievement: Vol. 13. Motivating students, improving schools* (pp. 27–63). Greenwich, CT: JAI Press.

Andrade, H. L. (2019, August). *A critical review of research on student self-assessment.* Frontiers in Education. Retrieved from https://www.frontiersin.org/articles/10.3389/feduc.2019.00087/full

Arky, B. (n.d.). *How to help kids learn to fail.* Child Mind Institute. Retrieved from https://childmind.org/article/how-to-help-kids-learn-to-fail/#

Assor, A., Kaplan, H., & Roth, G. (2002). Choice is good, but relevance is excellent: Autonomy-enhancing and suppressing teacher behaviours predicting students' engagement in schoolwork. *British Journal of Educational Psychology, 72*(2), 261–278. doi:10.1348/000709902158883

Baker, J. A., Grant, S., & Morlock, L. (2008). The teacher-student relationship as a developmental context for children with internalizing or externalizing behavior problems. *School Psychology Quarterly, 23*(1), 3–15. doi:10.1037/1045-3830.23.1.3

Bandura, A. (1997). *Self-efficacy: The exercise of control.* New York: W. H. Freeman.

Barnette, J. (1994, July). *Evaluation of teacher classroom questioning behaviors.* Paper presented at the third Annual National Evaluation Institute, Gatlinburg, TN. Retrieved from https://files.eric.ed.gov/fulltext/ED377188.pdf

Barrington, K. (2020, November 5). How does bullying affect a student's academic performance [Blog post]. Retrieved from https://www.publicschoolreview.com/blog/how-does-bullying-affect-a-students-academic-performance

Barron, L., & Kinney, P. (2018). *Middle school: A place to belong and become.* Columbus, OH: Association for Middle Level Education.

Battistich, V., & Horn, A. (1997). The relationship between students' sense of their school as a community and their involvement in problem behaviors. *American Journal of Public Health, 87*(12), 1997–2001. doi:10.2105/AJPH.87.12.1997

Baumeister, R. F., DeWall, N., Ciarocco, N. J., & Twenge, J. M. (2005). Social exclusion impairs self-regulation. *Journal of Personality and Social Psychology, 88*(4), 589–604. doi:10.1037/0022-3514.88.4.589

Baumeister, R. F., & Leary, M. (1995). The need to belong: Desire for interpersonal attachments as a fundamental human motivation. *Psychological Bulletin, 117*(3), 497–529. doi:10.1037/0033-2909.117.3.497

Baumeister, R. F., Twenge, J. M., & Nuss, C. K. (2002). Effects of social exclusion on cognitive processes: Anticipated aloneness reduces intelligent thought. *Journal of Personality and Social Psychology, 83*(4), 817–827. doi:10.1037/0022-3514.83.4.817

Berckemeyer, J. (2017). *Managing the madness: A practical guide to middle grades classrooms.* Columbus, OH: Association for Middle Level Education.

Berman, S. (1997). *Children's social consciousness and the development of social responsibility. SUNY series: Democracy and education.* Albany: State University of New York Press.

Bierman, K. L. (2004). *Peer rejection: Developmental processes and intervention strategies.* New York: Guilford.

Birch, S. H., & Ladd, G. W. (1998). Children's interpersonal behaviors and the teacher–child relationship. *Developmental Psychology, 34*(5), 934–946. doi:10.1037/0012-1649.34.5.934

Blackhart, G. C., Nelson, B. C., Winter, A., & Rockney, A. (2011). Self-control in relation to feelings of belonging and acceptance. *Self and Identity, 10*, 152–165. doi:10.1080/15298861003696410

Blad, E. (2017, June 20). Students' sense of belonging at school is important. It starts with teachers. *EdWeek.* Retrieved from https://www.edweek.org/ew/articles/2017/06/21/belonging-at-school-starts-with-teachers.html

Blankstein, A. M. (2009). *Failure is not an option: 6 principles that advance student achievement in highly effective school* (3rd ed.). Thousand Oaks, CA: Corwin.

Blum, R., & Libbey, H. P. (2004). School connectedness: Strengthening health and education outcomes for teens. *Journal of School Health, 74*(7), 229–299.

Blum, R. W., McNeely, C. A., & Rinehart, P. M. (2002). *Improving the odds: The untapped power of schools to improve the health of teens.* Minneapolis: Center for Adolescent Health and Development, University of Minnesota. Retrieved from http://www.sfu.ca/cfrj/fulltext/blum.pdf

Breiseth, L. (2016, February). Getting to know ELLs' families. *Educational Leadership, 73*(5), 46–50. Retrieved from http://www.ascd.org/publications/educational-leadership/feb16/vol73/num05/Getting-to-Know-ELLs'-Families.aspx

Brooks, J. G., & Brooks, M. G. (1999). *In search of understanding: The case for constructivist classrooms* (Revised ed.). Alexandria, VA: ASCD.

Bryk, A. S., & Schneider, B. (2002). *Trust in schools: A core resource for improvement.* New York: Russell Sage Foundation.

Burkhardt, R. (2003). *Writing for real: Strategies for engaging adolescent writers.* Portsmouth, NH: Stenhouse.

Card, N. A., & Hodges, E. V. (2008). Peer victimization among schoolchildren: Correlations, causes, consequences, and considerations in assessment and intervention. *School Psychology Quarterly, 23*(4), 451–461. doi:10.1037/a0012769

CASEL. (2020a). *Core SEL competencies.* Retrieved from https://casel.org/core-competencies/

CASEL. (2020b). *Overview of SEL.* Retrieved from https://casel.org/overview-sel/

Cook-Sather, A. (2006). Sound, presence, and power: "Student voice" in educational research and reform. *Curriculum Inquiry, 36,* 359–390. doi:10.1111/j.1467-873X.2006.00363.x

Deci, E. L., & Ryan, R. M. (1987). The support of autonomy and the control of behavior. *Journal of Personality and Social Psychology, 53*(6), 1024–1037. doi:10.1037/0022-3514.53.6.1024

Decker, D. M., Dona, D. P., & Christenson, S. L. (2007). Behaviorally at-risk African American students: The importance of student–teacher relationships for student outcomes. *Journal of School Psychology, 45,* 83–109. doi:10.1016/j.jsp.2006.09.004

DeGeneres, E. (2011). *Seriously . . . I'm kidding.* New York: Hatchette Book Group.

de Ridder, D., Lensvelt-Mulders, G., Finkenauer, C., Stok, F., & Baumeister, R. (2012). Taking stock of self-control: A meta-analysis of how trait self-control relates to a wide range of behaviors. *Personality and Social Psychology Review, 16*(1), 76–99. doi:10.1177/1088868311418749

Derosier, M. E., & Newcity, J. (2005). Students' perceptions of the school climate: Implications for school safety. *Journal of School Violence, 4*(3), 3–20. doi:10.1300/J202v04n03_02

DeWall, N., Deckman, T., Pond, R. S., & Bonser, I. (2011). Belongingness as a core personality trait: How social exclusion influences functioning and personality expression. *Journal of Personality, 79*(6), 1281–1314. doi:10.1111/j.1467-6494.2010.00695.x

Doherty, J. (2017). Skilful questioning: The beating heart of good pedagogy. *Impact.* Retrieved from https://impact.chartered.college/article/doherty-skilful-questioning-beating-heart-pedagogy/

Durlak, J. A., Weissberg, R. P., Dymnicki, A. B., Taylor, R. D., & Schellinger, K. B. (2011). The impact of enhancing students' social and emotional learning: A meta-analysis of school-based universal interventions. *Child Development, 82*(1), 405–432. doi:10.1111/j.1467-8624.2010.01564.x

Dusenbury, L., & Weissberg, R. P. (2017). *Social emotional learning in elementary school.* University Park: Pennsylvania State University.

Dweck, C. S. (2007). *Mindset: The new psychology of success.* New York: Random House.

Eccles, J. S., & Wigfield, A. (1995). In the mind of the actor: The structure of adolescents' achievement task values and expectancy-related beliefs. *Personality and Social Psychology Bulletin, 21,* 215–225. doi:10.1177/0146167295213003

Elledge, L. C., Elledge, A. R., Newgent, R. A., & Cavell, T. A. (2016). Social risk and peer victimization in elementary school children: The protective role of teacher-student relationships. *Journal of Abnormal Child Psychology, 44*(4), 691–703. doi:10.1007/s10802-015-0074-z

Erie, T. M., & Topolinski, S. (2017), The grounded nature of psychological perspective-taking. *Journal of Personality and Social Psychology, 112*(5), 683–695. doi:10.1037/pspa0000081

Felitti, V. J., Anda, R. F., Nordenberg, D., Williamson, D. F., Spitz, A. M., Edwards, V., . . . Marks, J. S. (1998). Relationship of childhood abuse and household dysfunction to many of the leading causes of death in adults. The adverse childhood experiences (ACE) study. *American Journal of Preventive Medicine, 14*(4), 245–258. doi:10.1016/S0749-3797(98)00017-8

Fielding, M. (2004). Transformative approaches to student voice: Theoretical underpinnings, recalcitrant realities. *British Educational Research Journal, 30*(2), 295–311. doi:10.1080/0141192042000195236

Flutter, J. (2007). Teacher development and pupil voice. *Curriculum Journal, 18*(3), 343–354. doi:10.1080/09585170701589983

Flutter, J., & Ruddick, J. (2004). *Consulting pupils: What's in it for schools?* New York: Routledge Falmer.

Furrer, C., & Skinner, E. (2003). Sense of relatedness as a factor in children's academic engagement and performance. *Journal of Educational Psychology, 95*(1), 148–162. doi:10.1037/0022-0663.95.1.148

Galinsky, A. D., & Moskowitz, G. B. (2000). Perspective-taking: Decreasing stereotype expression, stereotype accessibility, and in-group favoritism. *Journal of Personality and Social Psychology, 78*(4), 708–724. doi:10.1037/0022-3514.78.4.708

Gehlbach, H. (2017). Learning to walk in another's shoes. *Phi Delta Kappan, 98*(6), 8–12. doi:10.1177/0031721717696471

Gehlbach, H., Marietta, G., King, A., Karutz, C., Bailenson, J. N., & Dede, C. (2015). Many ways to walk a mile in another's moccasins: Type of social perspective taking and its effect on negotiation outcomes. *Computers in Human Behavior, 52,* 523–532. doi:10.1016/j.chb.2014.12.035

Gillies, R. M. (2008). The effects of cooperative learning on junior high school students' behaviours, discourse and learning during a science-based learning activity. *School Psychology International, 29,* 328–347. doi:10.1177/0143034308093673

Gillies, R. M. (2014). Cooperative learning: Developments in research. *International Journal of Educational Psychology, 3*(2), 125–140.

Gillies, R. M., & Haynes, M. (2011). Increasing explanatory behavior, problem-solving, and reasoning within classes using cooperative group work. *Instructional Science, 39*(3), 349–366. doi:10.1007/s11251-010-9130-9

Goodenow, C. (1993a). Classroom belonging among early adolescent students: Relationships to motivation and achievement. *Journal of Early Adolescence, 13*(1), 21–43. doi:10.1177/0272431693013001002

Goodenow, C. (1993b). The psychological sense of school membership among adolescents: Scale development and educational correlates. *Psychology in the Schools, 30*(1), 79–90. doi:10.1002/1520-6807(199301)30:1<79::AID-PITS2310300113>3.0.CO;2-X

Goodenow, C., & Grady, K. (1993). The relationship of school belonging and friends' values to academic motivation among urban adolescent students. *Journal of Experimental Education, 62*(1), 60–71. doi:10.1080/00220973.1993.9943831

Hamre, B. K., & Pianta, R. C. (2001). Early teacher–child relationships and the trajectory of children's school outcomes through eighth grade. *Child Development, 72*(2), 625–638. doi:10.1111/1467-8624.00301

Hawker, D. S., & Boulton, M. J. (2000). Twenty years' research on peer victimization and psychosocial maladjustment: A meta-analytic review of cross-sectional studies. *Journal of Child Psychology and Psychiatry, 41*(4), 441–455. doi:10.1111/1469-7610.00629

Hu, M. (2008). Promoting positive peer relationships. In M. Hu & W. Li (Eds.), *Classroom management: Creating a positive learning environment.* Hong Kong: Hong Kong University Press.

Huang, F. L., Lewis, C., Cohen, D. R., Prewett, S., & Herman, K. (2018) Bullying involvement, teacher–student relationships, and psychosocial outcomes. *School Psychology Quarterly, 33*(2), 223–234. doi:10.1037/spq0000249

International Institute for Restorative Practices. (2020). *What is restorative practices?* Retrieved from https://www.iirp.edu/restorative-practices/what-is-restorative-practices.

Johnson, D., & Johnson, R. (1990). Cooperative learning and achievement. In S. Sharan (Ed.), *Cooperative learning: Theory and research* (pp. 23–37). New York: Praeger.

Johnson, D., & Johnson, R. (2009). An educational psychology success story: Social interdependence theory and cooperative learning. *Educational Researcher, 38*(5), 365–379.

Johnson, D., & Johnson, R. (2020). *An overview of cooperative learning.* Retrieved from http://www.co-operation.org/what-is-cooperative-learning

Johnson, D. W., Johnson, R. T., & Holubec, E. J. (2008). *Cooperation in the classroom* (8th ed.). Edina, MN: Interaction.

Juvonen, L. (2006). Sense of belonging, social bonds, and school functioning. In P. A. Alexander & P. H. Winne (Eds.), *Handbook of educational psychology* (2nd ed., pp. 255–674). Mahwah, NJ: Lawrence Erlbaum.

Kagan, S. (1988). *Cooperative learning: Resources for teachers.* Riverside: University of California.

Katz, I., & Assor, A. (2007). When choice motivates and when it does not. *Educational Psychology Review, 19*(4), 429–442. doi:10.1007/s10648-006-9027-y

Kemple, K. M., & Hartle, L. C. (1997). Getting along: How teachers can support children's peer relationships. *Early Childhood Education Journal, 24*(3), 139–146. doi:10.1007/BF02353270

Kim, W. C., & Mauborgne, R. (2003). Fair process: Managing in the knowledge economy. *Harvard Business Review, 75*(4), 65–75.

Kinney, P. (2012). *Fostering student accountability through student-led conferences.* Columbus, OH: Association for Middle Level Education.

Klem, A. M., & Connell, J. P. (2004). Relationships matter: Linking teacher support to student engagement and achievement. *Journal of School Health, 74*(7), 262–273.

Knost, L. R. (2017, February 8). *Peaceful parenting resources.* [Facebook post]. Retrieved from https://www.facebook.com/littleheartsbooks/posts/taking-care-of-yourself-doesnt-mean-me-first-it-means-me-too-you-matter-your-hap/1368060613224539/

Konishi, C., Hymal, S., Zumbo, B. D., & Zhen, L. (2010). Do school bullying and student–teacher relationships matter for academic achievement? A multilevel analysis. *Canadian Journal of School Psychology, 25*(1), 19–39. doi:10.1177/0829573509357550

Konishi, C., & Wong, T. (2018). Relationships and school success: From a social-emotional learning perspective. In B. Bernal-Morales (Ed.), *Health and academic achievement* (pp. 103–122). Rijeka, Croatia: InTech.

Korinek, L., Walther-Thomas, C., McLaughlin, V., & Williams, B. (1999). Creating classroom communities and networks for student support. *Intervention in School and Clinic, 35,* 3–8. doi:10.1177/105345129903500101

Kulik, J. A., & Kulik, C. C. (1988). Timing of feedback and verbal learning. *Review of Educational Research, 58*(1), 79–97. doi:10.3102/00346543058001079

Ladd, B., & Wardrop, J. L. (2001). Chronicity and instability of children's peer victimization experience as predictors of loneliness and school satisfaction trajectories. *Child Development, 72*(1), 134–151. doi:10.1111/1467-8624.00270

Lee, R. M., & Robbins, S. B. (1998). The relationship between social connectedness and anxiety, self-esteem, and social identity. *Journal of Counseling Psychology, 45*(3), 338–345.

Leets, L., & Wolf, S. (2005). Adolescent rules for social exclusion: When is it fair to exclude someone else? *Journal of Moral Education, 34*(3), 343–362. doi:10.1080/03057240500211618

Li, Y., Lynch, A. D., Kalvin, C., Liu, J., & Lerner, J. (2011). Peer relationships as a context for the development of school engagement during early adolescence. *International Journal of Behavioral Development, 35,* 329–342. doi:10.1177/0165025411402578

Libbey, H. P. (2004). Measuring student relationships to school: Attachment, bonding, connectedness, and engagement. *Journal of School Health, 74*(7), 275–283. doi:10.1111/j.1746-1561.2004.tb08284.x

Libbey, H. P. (2007). *School connectedness: Influence above and beyond family connectedness.* Ann Arbor: University of Michigan ProQuest Information and Learning Company.

Lou, Y., Abrami, P. C., Spence, J. C., Poulsen, C., Chambers, B., & d'Apollonia, S. (1996). Within-class grouping: A meta-analysis. *Review of Educational Research, 66*(4), 423–458. doi:10.3102/00346543066004423

Loukas, A., Roalson, L. A., & Herrera, D. E. (2010). School connectedness buffers the effects of negative family relations and poor effortful control on early adolescent conduct problems. *Journal of Research on Adolescence, 20*(1), 13–22. doi:10.1111/j.1532-7795.2009.00632.x

Maddox, S., & Prinz, R. J. (2003). School bonding in children and adolescents: Conceptualization, assessment, and associated variables. *Clinical Child and Family Psychology Review, 6*(1), 31–49. doi:10.1023/A:1022214022478

Marzano, R. J., Marzano, J. S., & Pickering, D. J. (2003). *Classroom management that works.* Alexandria, VA: ASCD.

Maslow, A. (1968). *Toward a psychology of being* (2nd ed.). New York: Van Nostrand Reinhold.

Mayfield, V. (2020). *Cultural competence now: 56 exercises to help educators understand and challenge bias, racism, and privilege.* Alexandria, VA: ASCD.

McCoy, V. (2020, July 14). *How formative assessment boosts metacognition—and learning.* Northwest Evaluation Association. Retrieved from https://www.nwea.org/blog/2020/how-formative-assessment-boosts-metacognition-and-learning/

McCracken, P. (2005). Cooperative learning as a classroom management strategy. *Momentum, 36,* 10–12.

McMillan, J. H., & Hearn, J. (2008). Student self-assessment: The key to stronger student motivation and higher achievement. *Educational Horizons, 87*(1), 40–49.

McNamara, K. (1996). Bonding to school and the development of responsibility. *Journal of Emotional and Behavioral Problems, 4*(4), 33–35.

McNeely, C., Nonnemaker, J. M., & Blum, R. (2002). Promoting school connectedness: Evidence from the National Longitudinal Study of Adolescent Health. *Journal of School Health, 72*(4), 138–146. doi:10.1111/j.1746-1561.2002.tb06533.x

Murray, C., & Malmgren, K. (2005). Implementing a teacher–student relationship program in a high-poverty urban school: Effects on social, emotional, and academic adjustment and lessons learned. *Journal of School Psychology, 43*(2), 137–152. doi:10.1016/j.jsp.2005.01.003

Nike. (2012, December 8). Michael Jordan "failure" commercial [Video file]. Retrieved from https://www.youtube.com/watch?v=JA7G7AV-LT8

O'Connor, E., Dearing, E., & Collins, B. A. (2011). Teacher–child relationship and behavior problem trajectories in elementary school. *American Educational Research Journal, 48,* 120–162. doi:10.3102/0002831210365008

O'Neel, C. G., & Fuligni, A. (2013). A longitudinal study of school belonging and academic motivation across high school. *Child Development, 84*(2), 678–692. doi:10.1111/j.1467-8624.2012.01862.x

Operation Respect. (n.d.). Don't laugh at me [Video file]. Retrieved from https://operationrespect.org/get-inspired/videos/

Osterman, K. F. (2000). Students' need for belonging in the school community. *Review of Educational Research, 70*(3), 323–367. doi:10.3102/00346543070003323

Osterman, K. F. (2010). Teacher practice and students' sense of belonging. In T. Lovat, N. Clement, & R. Toomey (Eds.), *International research handbook on values education and student wellbeing* (pp. 239–260). New York: Springer.

Pate, A. (2020). *The innocent classroom: Dismantling racial bias to support students of color.* Alexandria, VA: ASCD.

Pettigrew, T. F. (1998). Intergroup contact theory. *Annual Review of Psychology, 49*(1), 65–85. doi:10.1146/annurev.psych.49.1.65

Pettigrew, T. F., & Tropp, L. R. (2008). How does intergroup contact reduce prejudice? Meta-analytic tests of three mediators. *European Journal of Social Psychology, 38*(6), 922–934. doi:10.1002/ejsp.504

Pianta, R. C. (1999). *Enhancing relationships between children and teachers.* Washington, DC: American Psychological Association. doi:10.1037/10314-000

Puckett, D. (2005). *Mr. DeVore's do-over: A little story for teachers.* Columbus, OH: Association for Middle Level Education.

Resnick, M. D., Bearman, P. S., Blum, R. W., Bauman, K., Harris, K. M., Jones, J., . . . Udry, J. R. (1997). Protecting adolescents from harm. Findings from the National Longitudinal Study on Adolescent Health. *Journal of the American Medical Association, 278*(10), 823–832. doi:10.1001/jama.1997.03550100049038

Robers, S., Zhang, J., Truman, J., & Snyder, T. D. (2012). *Indicators of school crime and safety: 2011.* Washington, DC: U.S. Department of Education, U.S. Department of Justice, Office of Justice Programs. Retrieved from https://nces.ed.gov/pubs2012/2012002.pdf

Roeser, R. W., Midgley, C., & Urdan, T. C. (1996). Perceptions of the school psychological environment and early adolescents' psychological and behavioral functioning in school: The mediating role of goals and belonging. *Journal of Educational Psychology, 88*, 408–422. doi:10.1037/0022-0663.88.3.408

Roffey, S. (2012). Pupil wellbeing—teacher wellbeing: Two sides of the same coin? *Educational and Child Psychology, 29*(4), 8–17.

Rohrbeck, C. A., & Gray, L. S. (2014). Peer relationships: Promoting positive peer relationships during childhood. In T. Gullotta & M. Bloom (Eds.), *Encyclopedia of preventive and community psychology* (2nd ed., pp. 828–836). Berlin/Heidelberg: Springer SBM.

Rolheiser, C., & Ross, J. A. (2001). Student self-evaluation: What research says and what practice shows. In R. D. Small & A. Thomas (Eds.), *Plain talk about kids* (pp. 43–57). Covington, LA: Center for Development and Learning.

Rosenshine, B., Meister, C., & Chapman, S. (1996). Teaching students to generate questions: A review of the intervention studies. *Review of Educational Research, 66*, 181–221. doi:10.3102/00346543066002181

Roseth, C. J., Johnson, D. W., & Johnson, R. T. (2008). Promoting early adolescents' achievement and peer relationships: The effects of cooperative, competitive, and individualistic goal structures. *Psychological Bulletin, 134*(2), 223–246. doi:10.1037/0033-2909.134.2.223

Rotary International. (2020). *Guiding principles.* Retrieved from https://my.rotary.org/en/guiding-principles

Ryan, A. M., & Patrick, H. (2001). The classroom social environment and changes in adolescents' motivation and engagement during middle school. *American Educational Research Journal, 38*, 437–460. doi:10.3102/00028312038002437

Sadker, D., Sadker, M., & Zittleman, K. R. (2009). *Still failing at fairness: How gender bias cheats girls and boys in school and what we can do about it.* New York: Scribner.

Sapon-Shevin, M. (1994). Cooperative learning and middle schools: What would it take to really do it right? *Theory into Practice, 33*(3), 183. doi:10.1080/00405849409543637

Shochet, I. M., Dadds, M. R., Ham, D., & Montague, R. (2006). School connectedness is an underemphasized parameter in adolescent mental health: Results of a community prediction study. *Journal of Clinical Child & Adolescent Psychology, 35*(2), 170–179. doi:10.1207/s15374424jccp3502_1

Silver, R. B., Measelle, J. R., Armstrong, J. M, & Essex, M. J. (2005). Trajectories of classroom externalizing behavior: Contributions of child characteristics, family characteristics, and the teacher–child relationship during the school transition. *Journal of School Psychology, 43*(1), 39–60. doi:10.1016/j.jsp.2004.11.003

Slavin, R. E. (1991). *Student team learning: A practical guide to cooperative learning* (3rd ed.). Washington, DC: National Education Association. Retrieved from https://files.eric.ed.gov/fulltext/ED339518.pdf

Slavin, R. E. (1996). Research on cooperative learning and achievement: What we know, what we need to know. *Contemporary Educational Psychology, 21*(1), 43–69. doi:10.1006/ceps.1996.0004

Souers, K., & Hall, P. (2016). *Fostering resilient learners: Strategies for creating a trauma-sensitive classroom.* Alexandria, VA: ASCD.

Souers, K., & Hall, P. (2018). *Relationship, responsibility, and regulation: Trauma-invested practices for fostering resilient learners.* Alexandria, VA: ASCD.

Starecheski, L. (2015, March 2). *Take the ACE quiz—And learn what it does and doesn't mean.* National Public Radio. http://www.npr.org/sections/health-shots/2015/03/02/387007941/take-the-ace-quiz-and-learn-what-it-does-and-doesnt-mean

Steinberg, L., & Monahan, C. (2007). Age differences in resistance to peer influence. *Developmental Psychology, 43*(6), 1531–1543. doi:10.1037/0012-1649.43.6.1531

Strudwicke, L. (2000). *Sense of belonging and self-esteem: What are the implications for educational outcomes of secondary school students? A literature review* (Bachelor's thesis, Edith Cowan University). Retrieved from https://ro.ecu.edu.au/theses_hons/867/

Tangney, J., Baumeister, R., & Boone, A. (2004). High self-control predicts good adjustment, less pathology, better grades, and interpersonal success. *Journal of Personality, 72*, 271–324. doi:10.1111/j.0022-3506.2004.00263.x

Teasley, M. L. (2014). Shifting from zero tolerance to restorative justice in schools. *Children & Schools, 36*(3), 131–133. doi:10.1093/cs/cdu016

Twenge, J. M., Baumeister, R. F., DeWall, C. N., Ciarocco, N. J., & Bartels, J. M. (2007). Social exclusion decreases prosocial behavior. *Journal of Personality and Social Psychology, 92*(1), 56–66. doi:10.1037/0022-3514.92.1.56

U.S. Centers for Disease Control and Prevention. (2009). *School connectedness: Strategies for increasing protective factors among youth.* Atlanta: U.S. Department of Health and Human Services.

U.S. Department of Health and Human Services. (2020, August). Facts about bullying. Retrieved from https://www.stopbullying.gov/resources/facts

Walton, G. (2005). Bullying widespread: A critical analysis of research and public discourse on bullying. *Journal of School Violence, 4*(1), 91–118. doi:10.1300/J202v04n01_06

Wang, M., & Holcombe, R. (2010). Adolescents' perceptions of school environment, engagement, and academic achievement in middle school. *American Educational Research Journal, 47*(3), 633–662. doi:10.3102/0002831209361209

Wachtel, T., & McCold, P. (2004, August 5). *From restorative justice to restorative practices: Expanding the paradigm.* IIRP News. Retrieved from https://www.iirp.edu/news/from-restorative-justice-to-restorative-practices-expanding-the-paradigm

Wells, A. S., Fox, L., & Cordova-Cobo, D. (2016, February 9). *How racially diverse schools and classrooms can benefit all students: Report from the Century Foundation.* Retrieved from https://tcf.org/content/report/how-racially-diverse-schools-and-classrooms-can-benefit-all-students/?agreed=1

Wentzel, K. R., & Caldwell, K. (1997). Friendships, peer acceptance, and group membership: Relations to academic achievement in middle school. *Child Development, 68*(6), 1198–1209. doi:10.2307/1132301

White, S. (2012, January 9). *Time to think: Using restorative questions.* IIRP News. Retrieved from https://www.iirp.edu/news/time-to-think-using-restorative-questions

Wilen, W. W. (1991). *Questioning skills for teachers: What research says to the teacher* (3rd ed.). Washington, DC: National Education Association.

Wilkinson, I. A., & Fung, I. Y. (2002). Small-group composition and peer effects. *International Journal of Educational Research, 37*(5), 425–447. doi:10.1016/S0883-0355(03)00014-4

Winfrey, O. (2017, October 10). FAILURE is just an experience! [Video file.] Retrieved from https://www.youtube.com/watch?v=Xxf4CHDNBQ4

Wingspread. (2004). Wingspread declaration on school connections. *Journal of School Health, 74*(7), 233–234. doi:10.1111/j.1746-1561.2004.tb08279.x

Wormeli, R. (2011, November). Redos and retakes done right. *Educational Leadership, 69*(3), 22–26.

Wormeli, R. (2013, August). *Looking at executive function.* Association for Middle Level Education. Retrieved from https://www.amle.org/BrowsebyTopic/WhatsNew/WNDet/TabId/270/ArtMID/888/ArticleID/298/Looking-at-Executive-Function.aspx

Zimmerman, B. J., & Schunk, D. H. (2011). *Handbook of self-regulation of learning and performance.* New York: Routledge.

Index

The letter *f* following a page locator denotes a figure.

About the Authors

**Laurie Barron** is superintendent of the Evergreen School District in Kalispell, Montana, and was named 2021 Montana Superintendent of the Year. Over the past 25 years, she has served as a high school English teacher and coach, a middle school assistant principal, and a middle school principal. She has served as a part-time assistant professor at the university level.

Laurie is a National Board–certified teacher and has been honored as a Teacher of the Year and STAR Teacher. She was 2012 Georgia Principal of the Year and 2013 MetLife/NASSP National Middle Level Principal of the Year. As a superintendent, Laurie has been recognized as 2020 Northwest Montana Regional Superintendent of the Year and 2019 Empowered Superintendent of the Year (Montana Educational Technologists Association). She received the 2018 G. V. Erickson Award, which is given to a member of the School Administrators of Montana who has made the greatest contribution to the betterment of education in the state. She is co-author of the books *What Parents Need to Know About Common Core and Other College- and Career-Ready Standards* and *Middle School: A Place to Belong and Become* and has authored numerous articles on education. She is also a speaker who provides motivation and professional learning to teachers and administrators throughout the United States.

Laurie is living the dream in Whitefish, Montana, with her husband, Daniel, and their high school–aged daughter, Emma. Together they enjoy watching Georgia Bulldogs football, snow skiing, hiking, camping, and rafting (and supporting Emma in her many athletic activities). Laurie may be reached at lauriebarron18@gmail.com. Follow her on Twitter: @LaurieBarron.

Patti Kinney speaks, presents, and consults on middle-level education issues at the national and international levels. She began her career as an elementary music specialist and has taught 5th and 6th grades in an elementary school and 6th and 7th grades in a middle school setting. She has been involved in district staff development work and has taught a variety of instructional and management skills classes for adults. During a one-year sabbatical, she also taught in the education department of Southern Oregon University. As an assistant principal and later principal of Talent Middle School, Patti was involved in the process of transforming a grades 7–8 junior high school into a grades 6–8 middle school. In 2000, the school was recognized as one of "100 highly successful middle schools" in a national research study sponsored by the National Association of Secondary School Principals (NASSP).

Patti is a past president of the Association for Middle Level Education and of the Oregon Middle Level Association. In 1996, she was Oregon Assistant Principal of the Year; in 2003, she was both Oregon Principal of the Year and the MetLife/NASSP National Middle Level Principal of the Year. From 2007 to 2014, she lived in Reston, Virginia, and served as Associate Director of Middle Level Services for the NASSP. She is the author of *Fostering Student Accountability Through Student-Led Conferences* and co-author of *Voices of Experience: Perspectives from Successful Middle Level Leaders*; *The What, Why, and How of Student-Led Conferences*; *What Parents Need to Know About Common Core and Other College- and Career-Ready Standards*; and *Middle School: A Place to Belong and Become*. She has also published numerous education articles, including regular pieces in NASSP's *Principal Leadership*.

Patti recently married Dan Bolton (whom she has known since 1st grade) and relocated from southern Oregon to Cottage Grove, Oregon, where she grew up. Patti may be reached at kinneypatti@gmail.com. Follow her on Twitter: @pckinney.

Related ASCD Resources: Classroom Management

At the time of publication, the following resources were available (ASCD stock numbers in parentheses):

Affirmative Classroom Management: How do I develop effective rules and consequences in my school? (ASCD Arias) by Richard L. Curwin (#SF114042)

Better Behavior Practices (Quick Reference Guide) by Dominique Smith, Nancy Frey, Douglas Fisher, and Lee Ann Jung (#QRG120049)

Better Than Carrots or Sticks: Restorative Practices for Positive Classroom Management by Dominique Smith, Douglas Fisher, and Nancy Frey (#116005)

Classroom Management That Works: Research-Based Strategies for Every Teacher by Robert J. Marzano, Jana S. Marzano, and Debra Pickering (#103027)

Discipline with Dignity: How to Build Responsibility, Relationships, and Respect in Your Classroom, 4th Edition by Richard L. Curwin, Allen Mendler, and Brian Mendler (#118018)

From Behaving to Belonging: The Inclusive Art of Supporting Students Who Challenge Us by Julia Causton and Kate MacLeod (#121011)

Managing 21st Century Classrooms: How do I avoid ineffective classroom management practices? (ASCD Arias) by Jane Bluestein (#SF114046)

Managing Your Classroom with Heart: A Guide for Nurturing Adolescent Learners by Katy Ridenour (#107013)

Managing Your Classroom with Restorative Practices (Quick Reference Guide) by Dominique Smith, Douglas Fisher, and Nancy Frey (#QRG117093)

For up-to-date information about ASCD resources, go to www.ascd.org. You can search the complete archives of *Educational Leadership* at www.ascd.org/el.

For more information, send an email to member@ascd.org; call 1-800-933-2723 or 703-578-9600; send a fax to 703-575-5400; or write to Information Services, ASCD, 1703 N. Beauregard St., Alexandria, VA 22311-1714 USA.

WHOLE CHILD
TENETS

THE WHOLE CHILD

The ASCD Whole Child approach is an effort to transition from a focus on narrowly defined academic achievement to one that promotes the long-term development and success of all children. Through this approach, ASCD supports educators, families, community members, and policymakers as they move from a vision about educating the whole child to sustainable, collaborative actions.

We Belong relates to the **safe, supported,** and **engaged** tenets.

*For more about the ASCD Whole Child approach, visit **www.ascd.org/wholechild**.*

 1 HEALTHY
Each student enters school healthy and learns about and practices a healthy lifestyle.

2 SAFE
Each student learns in an environment that is physically and emotionally safe for students and adults.

 3 ENGAGED
Each student is actively engaged in learning and is connected to the school and broader community.

 4 SUPPORTED
Each student has access to personalized learning and is supported by qualified, caring adults.

 5 CHALLENGED
Each student is challenged academically and prepared for success in college or further study and for employment and participation in a global environment.